An Extremist for Love & Justice

Selected Sermons & Other Writings 2001-2010

Cynthia L. Landrum

Cover Photos copyright © Christopher Jensen, 2011, used with permission.

"The Paradox of Faith" originally printed in The Gardner News, Gardner, MA, December 14-15, 2002. Reprinted with permission.

"Responding with Love" originally printed as "People of Faith Respond with Love" in The Jackson Citizen Patriot; Jackson, MI; August 10, 2008. Reprinted with permission.

"The Name of God" originally printed in The Gardner News, Gardner, MA, January 18-19,2003. Reprinted with permission.

"If There Is a God..." originally printed in The UU World Magazine; Unitarian Universalist Association: Boston, MA; Winter 2009. Reprinted with permission.

"The Religious Importance of Tolerance" originally printed in The Gardner News, Gardner, MA, January 11-12, 2003. Reprinted with permission.

"Same-Sex Marriage" is reprinted from The Fitchburg Sentinel & Enterprise, with permission from MediaNews Group; February 4, 2004.

"Standing on the Side of Love This Valentine's Day" originally appeared as "State must recognize committed same-sex couples" in the Jackson Citizen Patriot; Jackson, MI; February 10, 2010. Reprinted with permission.

"Of Love and Marriage" originally appeared as "A wedding of adventure" in The Gardner News; Gardner, MA; February 22-23, 2003. Reprinted with permission.

"The Gaping Chasm" originally printed in The Gardner News; Gardner, MA; March 15-16, 2003. Reprinted with permission.

ISBN: 1-4610-7941-1
ISBN-13: 9781461079415

Dedication

For my daughter, Cathleen.

With thanks to my husband, Peter Morrison, for his love & support; my sister, Carrie Landrum, for her help and her own peace work; my father, William Landrum, for his help and inspiration; and the Universalist Unitarian Church of East Liberty for the gift of time and for walking this path of faith with me.

Contents

Introduction

But though I was initially disappointed at being categorized as an extremist, as I continued to think about the matter I gradually gained a measure of satisfaction from the label. Was not Jesus an extremist for love: "Love your enemies, bless them that curse you, do good to them that hate you, and pray for them which despitefully use you, and persecute you." Was not Amos an extremist for justice: "Let justice roll down like waters and righteousness like an ever flowing stream." Was not Paul an extremist for the Christian gospel: "I bear in my body the marks of the Lord Jesus." Was not Martin Luther an extremist: "Here I stand; I cannot do otherwise, so help me God." And John Bunyan: "I will stay in jail to the end of my days before I make a butchery of my conscience." And Abraham Lincoln: "This nation cannot survive half slave and half free." And Thomas Jefferson: "We hold these truths to be self evident, that all men are created equal…" So the question is not whether we will be extremists, but what kind of extremists we will be. Will we be extremists for hate or for love? Will we be extremists for the preservation of injustice or for the extension of justice?

—Martin Luther King, Jr.
From "Letter from the Birmingham Jail"

At some point while attending seminary, studying to become a Unitarian Universalist minister, I heard someone say, "Every minister has one sermon that they preach over and over again." As I gathered sermons together for this collection, I realized that it may have taken some time to distill my core message, but it has clearly emerged. My message is one of love and justice.

The first and most important part of my core message is love. Love, for me, is almost synonymous with faith. Faith and belief are something we have against all odds—I often quote Cornel West on this subject. Love is also something we have against all odds, I might say. It's hard to explain just what I mean about that, except to say a Universalist all-inclusive love is in some ways so improbable, and, like faith and belief, it can't be proven. It's what my faith rests in, certainly, but more than that, in the same way we say "God is Love" so repeatedly in Universalist-heritage churches, Faith is Love for me.

In some ways, I became an atheist and then later an agnostic because of love. Originally, since the God our larger culture, though not my church, was always talking about was a God who damned souls to Hell, I rejected God and declared myself an atheist. Later I reasoned that if there was a God, and that God was a loving God, then God would not damn people forever for not believing in God. Ultimately, this is Universalism, as I would later understand. While I didn't, from there, declare myself a theist but rather an agnostic, understanding the Universalist God of Love led me to be open to the possibility of God, to feel comfortable in the use of God language, and to be comfortable in the space in the middle, where sometimes God's presence seems more certain, and sometimes a world without God makes more sense.

In this volume I use God-language at times that makes it appear that I am a theist, rather than an agnostic. Sometimes that's because of the audience I was writing the original piece for, but sometiems its because the word "God" for me has come to mean things like Love and Justice, and those things I'm not agnostic about. I'm a true believer in Love and Justice.

I'm still agnostic about God, as I wrote in an article for the *UU World* that appears in this volume, but I do know that I believe that if there is a God then it is this Universalist God of Love. Furthermore, whether or not there is something we might term God, there is love. That love is what I believe in focusing on for the here and now. My spirituality of right relationship, which I go into further in many of the sermons, is about having that loving connection on many levels—personal, societal, global.

It may seem that I'm repeating myself in some of these sermons. It is no illusion. I am. One of the interesting things for me in pulling these together was that I was able to see the consistency of my faith. The core elements come up repeatedly in these writings—a Universalism-based agnosticism rooted in the inherent worth and dignity of all people, a spirituality of relationship that covers many spheres, a Christian legacy that influences me culturally and theologically, and an Earth-based sense of rhythm and ritual. In response to the question, "What's your theology?" I once described myself as something like a culturally-Christian, mystical earth-based agnostic humanist. All of that is still true, and I still use pieces of it in different contexts. But it can be summed up in one word: Love.

There are times when my sermons may not seem to be directly about love— they are about theology or church history or the meaning of life. But love is the root of all of this, and for me, the core of the faith that I explore in these sermons. "Where there is faith, there is love," the Hungarian Blessing used in one of our hymns states: "Hol hit—ott szeretet."

Go now and live your religion
Its truth reflect in all you do
Go, may love's presence ever guide you
Live the good life the whole day through.
—Author Unknown, Adapted by Ruth Smith

———

The second part of my core message is ultimately about justice and building the beloved community here on earth—a community that embodies this endless, eternal Love. At the Unitarian Universalist Church of East Liberty, in Clarklake, Michigan, where I serve, we end every service by singing to "Go now and live your religion." Guided by love, we are called to go out into the world to do the work of justice—faith, love, and justice are inextricably bound in the living faith of Unitarian Universalism. If my faith is love, justice is how I act out my faith.

There are a few issues I've returned to often—gay, lesbian, bisexual and transgender issues; interfaith issues, particularly our dealings with Islam in this society; poverty, healthcare, and other economic justice issues; feminist issues; and other issues of identity and civil rights.

For me, love and justice are completely intertwined. The implication of either a God with an all-pervasive love, or a world where Love is our guide, is a call to justice. The Unitarian minister Theodore Parker once spoke of the arc of the universe bending towards justice—a phrase picked up by both Martin Luther King, Jr. and Barack Obama. I believe this is true, and I believe it is love that bends the arc, or that love is the arc itself. What we are called to do is build the beloved community here on earth. The beloved community, obviously, is a community of love, but it is also a community of justice. If one loves the world with all one's mind and soul, I believe one wants a world with all her people treated with respect and dignity, and where the earth herself is cherished and protected.

Unitarian Universalist minister Richard Gilbert's book *The Prophetic Imperative* was required reading in seminary. It teaches of something very important to me: of justice work, and of doing that justice work through religious community. The causes that call me are varied—healthcare, immigration, same-sex marriage. However, they each relate to what I see as the core of our faith: our principle of respect for the inherent worth and dignity of every person.

I'm aware that there are some social justice issues, such as environmental issues and even peace, which I do not focus on as much. It may be hard to understand their omission for some individuals, as for some these issues are their passions and the most important of all. My calling has been to largely focus on social justice issues in the civil rights category. This is not to say that other issues aren't important, just that each person has personal passions, and these are mine.

As I talk to people of like minds who do not belong to a religious community, and who see no purpose in religion, I frequently cite social justice as one major purpose of religion. Even if your theology does not demand religious community, even if you have enough social connections elsewhere without religious community, liberal religious congregations, such as Unitarian Universalist congregations, are circles wherein we bring likeminded people together to work on issues of justice. Individual justice organizations do this for individual causes, but in liberal religion we have the flexibility to move from cause to cause and bring our voices and our numbers to this important work.

There are conservative voices in our movement who often say that if we stopped being so "political" we would grow more in numbers, and our faith could spread further. For me, without the social gospel, our faith is hollow. Whatever you believe, your beliefs have ramifications in how you act in the world. My beliefs do, and they demand that I preach on these subjects again and again until we build the beloved community here on earth.

———————

The writings I've included in this book are mostly sermons, but I've also incorporated some of my newspaper and magazine articles, as well as papers for my ministerial study group, the Ohio River Group.

Among the sermons are several "auction sermons" Like many churches, my church has an annual auction. Also, as many Unitarian Universalist ministers do at our church auctions, it has been my practice to donate a sermon topic of choice to the auction—the highest bidder on the sermon designates the topic for one of my sermons in the upcoming year.

In the beginning, I approached this with some trepidation, worried that people would ask me to preach on a subject that I was uncomfortable preaching about. I did give myself the right to refuse any topic. However, what has happened is that I've gotten some really wonderful topics that I might not have thought of otherwise. Some of these sermons have turned out to be favorites of members of the congregation. Indeed, they were all provocative, interesting topics resulting from deep questions the members of my church had been struggling with. The sermons "Vocation," "Where Do We Go from Here," "Everyday Heroism" and "To Not Live and Die in Vain" all were auction sermons.

———————

There are several themes, in addition to love and justice, that can be seen running through my writings. One is that many of my sermons use a work of literature as their subject. Like many Unitarian Universalists, and many in our ministry, I'm a lover of the written word. For this reason alone, I'll probably never become a preacher who works without a text. I have a deep love of the text.

I've always been an avid reader, something to which anyone who knew me growing up can attest. My house is overflowing with bookshelves. One of my family's stories about this is that when I was just learning to read my grandparents promised me a dollar for every book I read and put on a list for them that year. This was for books over and above what the teacher assigned. I turned in a list of thirty-some books. After that, despite the fact that they in every other way treated their grandchildren identically, they did not make this same offer to the younger grandchildren. After that, I had to resort to library summer reading programs for my reading awards, and filled up sheets and sheets with their stamps and stickers for each book I read.

From this childhood love of books, I went on to major in English literature in college, and then earned a Master's degree in English literature as well. To this day, I continue to teach English at the community college level. While teaching is another way to share my love of English language and literature, and brings me into contact with new non-fiction readings, I seldom find time these days to engage in a worthy piece of literature, and so when I do, I treasure it. One way to give myself permission to read literature is to preach on it, and so I do two things. First, I've made August my "pop culture month," where I often do sermons on movies and books, sometimes science fiction and fantasy, which has always been a love of mine. I haven't included any of the science fiction or fantasy-focused sermons here, but they are a lot of fun for me. Secondly, Jackson, Michigan had an NEA "Big Read" grant for a few years, and I've done a sermon in conjunction with the Big Read each of those years. With the Big Read we read *To Kill a Mockingbird*; *Bless Me, Ultima*; and *The Grapes of Wrath*, and some of these sermons are included in this volume.

In Unitarian Universalism, there is a concept of the "Loose-Leaf Bible," which means, for us, that our book of sacred scripture is not closed. We are always adding new writings to our canon, to what is sacred text for us. In seminary, we took a class on literature and theology, in which each student wrote a paper and presented it, arguing for inclusion of one particular text into the liberal canon. We heard papers on classics of literature, children's books, poetry, and non-fiction, as I recall.

In my personal "loose-leaf Bible," there is a lot of poetry, which is why I jumped at the chance to write a paper on poetry for my minister's study group, the

Ohio River Group, when we chose poetry as one year's topic (and I admit I submitted that topic to our brainstorming list).

––––––––

In my English composition courses, I tell my students that it is okay to use "I," but what I really dislike is the use of "You." I tell them not to address me, their reader, directly, because I might disagree with them about the thoughts or ideas they might attribute to me. It is a rule I break often in sermon writing—every good rule is meant to be broken. Thank *you* for picking up this volume and thank you for joining me in being an extremist for love and justice—together we build the beloved community.

Part 1
Faith in Love

Whose Are You?

October 10, 2010
Universalist Unitarian Church of East Liberty
Clarklake, MI

The Unitarian Universalist Minister's Group I'm in was having their annual fall meeting. They began by doing something I hate—they paired us off into dyads and asked us to discuss, for five minutes, our personal reactions to deep questions. One person was to ask, "Whose are you?" Then the other person would answer. The first would respond with, "May you be blessed with the knowledge of your true self." Then they would ask again, "Whose are you?" and do this on and on for five minutes as we explored the ways in which we are tied to this world, to whom we are responsible, the ways in which we're connected, to whom we belong: Whose are you? Whose are you? Whose are you? Whose are you? Whose are you?

I am, in a typical Unitarian Universalist fashion, instantly suspicious of this exercise. It smacks of an implied theism—that we're supposed to say, "I am God's." I suspect it to be just one more way in which humanists are being marginalized in our movement. Either we're being converted or ignored, I figure, by this crazy exercise.

But I'm here, and I have to do it, right? I'm the president of this group, after all, and if I revolt from the exercise, that will not be a good show of collegiality.

Joan looks at me. "Whose are you?" she asks, softly.

Well, I'm my family's. "May you be blessed with the knowledge of your true self. Whose are you?"

Well, I'm my congregation's. "May you be blessed with the knowledge of your true self. Whose are you?"

Suddenly, I remember. My mentor, the Rev. Dr. Andrew C. Kennedy—Drew—has talked about spirituality as a series of concentric circles that we must be in right relationship with, each coming with its ancient imperative.[1] These concentric circles of spiritual relationship have always resonated with me. I explore these relationships in response to Joan's questions.

I am my own—"to thine own self be true."

I am part my family's and friends' and the social groups to which I belong—love your neighbor.

I am society's—"feed the hungry, clothe the naked, shelter the homeless, care for the sick, welcome the stranger, and visit the imprisoned."

I am nature's; I am the earth's. Drew says, "The ancient imperative with respect to nature is to respect the environment and take only what we need."[2]

I am the cosmos'. Drew says:

> In traditional Western spiritual language, the ancient imperative in our relationship to the cosmos is to "Love thy God with all thy heart, and all thy soul, and all thy mind." In Buddhist terminology, the imperative is to "be present." In Taoist language, it is to be in harmony with the Tao. More simply, I think the ancient imperative here is to grow in wisdom.[3]

Then I responded, "I belong to the task, to the work of building right relationship and beloved community." "May you be blessed with the knowledge of your true self."

The question bounced back again—I am my own. "May you be blessed with the knowledge of your true self," Joan says. "Whose are you?" "That's it," I say, "That's all." No sooner do I say that then the chime rings.

When we get back to the larger group, of course, and we share all our answers, I realize all the other things to which I, too, belong—I belong to my colleagues; I belong to this faith tradition, the living tradition; I belong to the promise of the future; I belong to the heritage of the past. There are so many more things we could say. One woman says, "the starry, starry night." Yes, I think, I belong to that, too.

Whose are you? To whom do you belong? To what are you accountable? What calls you into being? Whose are you?

The faith I have, the faith I understand, is this faith that it is, somehow, important and meaningful to live and to love, that being in right relationship matters and is important, that "the arc of the universe bends towards justice," and that the greatest force is love. Love and justice and connection and right relationship—these are the rocks that I build my faith upon.

I suppose, when I think about the faiths that I don't understand—the faiths that say there is only one right path to what is holy and I know what it is and it is this, this vision of God in this kind of incarnation, and this scripture upon which I rest my faith, well, when you get right down to it these faiths are no more or less nonsensical than the faith that I myself hold—that love is more important than hate or fear. These things are faith—they are what we just simply believe. I don't know, and never have known, how to change someone's beliefs or change my own.

I've never had that profound conversion experience, nor witnessed it in someone nearby, and all the accounts I've read of it haven't made it any clearer.

In Buddhism, we hear of the Buddha sitting down under the bodhi tree and attaining enlightenment. He went through years of spiritual practice and meditation, of course, before he suddenly achieved enlightenment, but still we think of it as this powerful transformation moment. In Christianity, the story is that of Paul, then Saul, on the road to Damascus, when he hears God say, "Saul, why do you persecute me?"

It was something of an enlightening moment for me when I heard the Jesus Seminar scholars say that they don't believe, essentially, that Paul had this sort of moment of conversion to Christianity. They think Paul saw himself not as a convert to Christianity but as a Jew, and that this conversion story came later. They say Paul saw himself as a prophet, not a convert, in the style of the Old Testament prophets who talked about how the Jews have gone awry in their worship.[4]

But even if you do believe that, or anything else, I don't know or understand the conversion process—faith, belief, is what we believe in spite of all reason, because we feel it in our soul. You can't, for me, argue your way to faith. You can have a profound revelation, but how do you get to have one? For people who believe that you have to have faith to be saved, how do you get to there from where you are? How does faith happen? Nobody has ever been able to truly answer this—that I've found. Lots of people have answers—you have to be humble, you have to pray to God, you have to be open. That worked for them, I suppose. But I know there are humble, open people who have prayed and then—nothing.

It was interesting to find that the Jesus Seminar, by the way, doesn't believe that Paul said you have to have faith in Jesus. They say it is mistranslated—you don't have to have faith *in* Jesus, you have to have the faith *of* Jesus, or *like* Jesus. That is to say, Jesus was not the object of faith, in their opinion, but the model for it—you need to look at Jesus and learn from him how to have faith.

Well, if this is true, then Jesus tells us several things about how to have faith. He tells us to look at God like a parent, to pray to God like a father, Daddy, Abba. Jesus teaches, too, of humility—blessed are the meek, thy will be done, forgive us our trespasses.

But how, then, do we come by faith?

I think this is the wrong question. The question isn't how you believe, or how you come to believe it. The question really is what you believe and how you respond to it. This is an unpopular view in the postmodern era. I'm supposed to believe that any belief is as good as any other, right? I'm supposed to be so tolerant that I'm tolerant of intolerance, and so open to other religions that I think all religious beliefs are entirely equal.

Wrong.

Unitarian Universalist religious educator Sophia Lyon Fahs wrote in "It Matters What We Believe":

> Some beliefs are like walled gardens. They encourage exclusiveness, and the feeling of being especially privileged.
> Other beliefs are expansive and lead the way into wider and deeper sympathies....
> Some beliefs are divisive, separating the saved from the unsaved, friends from enemies.
> Other beliefs are bonds in a world community, where sincere differences beautify the pattern.
> Some beliefs are like blinders, shutting off the power to choose one's own direction.
> Other beliefs are like gateways opening wide vistas for exploration.[5]

She was absolutely right. It doesn't matter to me so much how you came by your faith as what you have faith *in*. It does matter what you believe. Truthfully, some beliefs *are* like walled gardens. Some beliefs are about hate and fear. An easy example of this is the Westboro Baptist Church, home of Fred Phelps, who bases his church on hate—his website URL includes the word hate. According to him, God hates lots of people and the greatest lie ever told was that God loves everybody. He believes God hates gay people, God hates the United States of America, God hates Muslims, and God hates Jews and Israel. That probably doesn't even begin to touch the list of who Fred Phelps thinks God hates.[6]

"Some beliefs are rigid, like the body of death, impotent in a changing world." It does matter what you believe.

It doesn't matter in these four walls if your beliefs are Christian, or Pagan, or Atheist. It doesn't matter if you believe in reincarnation or Heaven or Nirvana or dust. What matters is that you believe in love, and in justice, and in right relationship with your circles of spirituality. It matters that your beliefs are "expansive and lead the way into wider and deeper sympathies," that they are "like sunshine, blessing children with the warmth of happiness," that your beliefs are "bonds in a world community, where sincere differences beautify the pattern," and are "like gateways opening wide vistas for exploration." It matters that your beliefs "nurture self-confidence and enrich the feeling of personal worth," and that they are "pliable, like the young sapling, ever growing with the upward thrust of life." It matters what you believe.

Whose are you? You are love's. You are justice's. You are your neighbor's. You are God's or the Goddess' or the Cosmos'. And it matters.

Mother Wisdom: Humanism and the Goddess

April 6, 2008
Universalist Unitarian Church of Farmington, MI

For a long time, I've considered myself a humanist and an agnostic. However, what I want to share here is a very personal story about several experiences which made me realize that I had been limiting my understanding based on childish views of God. To start with, I do, even as a humanist agnostic, every so often, pray to God. I've called it, "keeping the lines of communication open, just in case he's up there." About four and a half years ago, I said a prayer that has become a memorable, and some would say mystical, experience for me.

I was at a Unitarian Universalist camp in New England, Rowe Camp, and I went on a walk to find a Goddess statue that I had heard about. I had the idea that I would climb into her lap and pray or reflect and it would be oh-so-spiritual. When I got there, her lap was small, she wasn't the Goddess image I had pictured, and her lap was full of snow and leaves and mud. I looked at her, then turned around and walked back. Halfway down to camp, I decided to pray. I put my hands against a large tree, and looked up, and started in my customary way: "Dear God, if you're up there..." I prayed and asked to be able to have a child. I said my amens, and stepped back, and promptly fell to the earth. I felt like I had been pushed to the earth. It seemed, to me, at the time, like it was a response to my prayer.

What did it mean? My first thoughts were that it was definitely negative. I thought maybe God was saying I was praying in the wrong way, or that the answer was no. But I wasn't sure.

Four years later, I figured it out. It took a trip across the world, a walk in a labyrinth, coming back, waiting a few months, another walk in a labyrinth, and a conversation with a Muslim woman friend to figure it out.

I was being dope-slapped by the Goddess. Now, I don't mean that literally, but I'll explain.

Ultimately, the answer to the prayer I spoke of earlier couldn't have been a simple "no," since I did have a child, but I worried about that up until her birth.

But after she was born, I put the experience behind me, and stopped really thinking about it. It was just one of those things, those indescribable, inexplicable moments, and it had no real impact on my theology.

Then, last June, I went to Transylvania for a conference for women ministers—American Unitarian Universalist, Transylvanian and British Unitarian, Dutch Remonstrant, and a couple of Hungarian reform ministers, and one of the things we did was walk in a labyrinth that was marked out on the floor with rope in the same room in which we worshipped. We did different exercises, such as walking in silence, walking while singing, and dancing through the labyrinth. Every morning and every evening there was also a dancing time where we did these sort of spiritual circle dances. My back was not up to so much dancing, so I often did a couple and then sat out. One day, near the end, I decided to walk the labyrinth while everyone else was dancing. I knew that the previous day the whole group had walked the labyrinth while asking a specific question as they walked. I had missed that exercise, since I had gone out with my sister's mother-in-law, who lives in Koloszvar, Romania, to see the town.

So I walked the labyrinth while the dancing was going on, and with each step I said a word of my question, rhythmically, over and over again, until I got to the center. The question was, "Is there a God?"

By way of background, I should say that periodically for the last, oh, say twenty-five years, I have prayed a prayer to God, asking if God is there, to give me some sort of sign and help me believe. I've never gotten a sign. But, as I say, "I try to keep the channels of communication open."

As I walked the labyrinth, I was completely absorbed in my question, in the rhythm of my question and my footsteps. The rest of the room, with the dancing, blurred out. So I got to the center of the labyrinth, paused, still asking my question, and turned around, and walked out, still asking the same question.

As I got towards the end stretch exiting, the room and the dancers came back into view. The women were all singing along with the song they were dancing to: "Ancient Mother, I hear you calling. Ancient Mother, I hear your song."

I realized it was an answer of sorts, and I had been asking the wrong question. I had long ago rejected my childhood image of God, the God who answers petitionary prayers, plays favorites in football games, saves some children and not others. I had long ago rejected the idea that there was an old man with a beard in the sky who looks down and watches and listens and reaches down and stirs things up every so often. But I had been continuing, whenever I prayed, to pray to that God. Even though I've studied theology, and I've preached on the subject, and I've led classes and written about feminist theology, in particular, and explored Pagan ritual—even though I've done all these things, I was still back in my childhood concept of prayer, doing the same kind of "Our father, who art in Heaven" kind of prayer.

Sometimes it is hard to let go of our childhood ideas of God. Other times, we rebel against that concept, but we don't replace it with anything else. I had broken down the theology, deconstructed the idea of God and patriarchy, but I had never reconstructed. Specifically, I have often said, "I don't know if there is a God, but I do have very specific ideas about what God is like if there is a God." I still believe it is true. But what I hadn't done is reconstructed my ritual, my prayer life, based on my understanding of theology. I was still doing petitionary prayer, still waiting for a literal, concrete answer from God.

Not much time had passed since the Transylvania trip when I went to a minister's retreat at the Grailville retreat center. It is a Catholic retreat center in Loveland, Ohio, where our Unitarian Universalist Ministers' Association chapter meets every year. It was also the site of the first conference for women ministers across the denomination.

In the back of the building I was staying in, they have a labyrinth. The paths are dirt paths dug through the tall grass. I decided to walk it one day. It was hot, so I carried my water bottle. I had decided to walk the labyrinth singing the song that I heard the women singing as I exited the labyrinth in Transylvania. "Ancient Mother, I hear you calling. Ancient Mother, I hear your song." Despite the water bottle in my hands, I held my hands in ritual position, palms down for walking in, letting go of things; palms up for walking out, receiving wisdom.

I walked the labyrinth while singing, stopping every so often for a swig of water. I wasn't watching my feet the whole time, and I almost stepped on a field mouse. He scurried away just in time. I think I saw a snake at one point, as well. The bugs and butterflies were all around. The grass was tall. I was sweating in the sun. I kept singing, very softly, almost like breathing, as my breath got harder and I got warmer.

I got to the center, and paused a moment in reflection, and then started out, still singing. As I came out, it came to me that I had been looking up, and looking around, and this labyrinth was calling me to look at the earth, to pay attention to the ground, to feel my connection to the world around me. All the sweat, my breathlessness, the field mouse, the butterflies, they were all telling me that I was part of the earth, it was part of me, and that the connection to the Ancient Mother, the way to hear her calling was not formal meditation or prayer, but living itself.

I thought back and put this together with a conversation I had had with a friend, a Muslim woman, a week or two before, and it all came together.

Shortly before I went to Grailville, I had lunch with a friend who had recently stopped wearing the hijab as part of her Muslim faith. She had undergone a spiritual transformation of sorts. She realized that the hijab represented dogma to her, and she no longer needed the dogma to be faithful. I had previously had conversations with her about the hijab, and she had said, as I've heard other women say, that it isn't restrictive or oppressive, and that it is a choice. As she came out from behind the veil, it was interesting to hear her say the opposite. She told me what it was like for her, after so many years of wearing it, to take it off and told be about her religious community's reaction. In the course of this conversation, I felt that she would be a sympathetic person to talk to about what I had experienced.

I talked with her about what I was processing from Transylvania, about how I had realized that when I've prayed to God in the past, I've prayed to exactly the sort of God that I know I don't believe in, even as a true agnostic. I don't believe that God/dess answers petitionary prayer—with both teams of the football game praying so hard, no game would ever end. I don't believe in a God/dess who interferes in human existence in that way. Yet that was the way I had still been praying to God, and when I prayed to God, I was praying to that same sort of Sistine Chapel old father God that I've even preached against. Therefore, when I asked, "Is there a God," and I heard "Ancient Mother, I hear you calling," it was telling me that prayer isn't supposed to be about me asking God/dess. Prayer is supposed to be about me listening to God/dess, and God/dess isn't going to give me a direct call. I know enough to know that. The song was saying I do hear the calling, even though it isn't literally God/dess saying, "Cindy, I want you to build an ark."

I still don't know, after all this, if there is a God/dess or not. But I knew then that it was time for me to revisit my understanding of God/dess, my understanding of prayer, my understanding of calling, of vocation.

What I believe, which is to say not what I know, but what I think holds truth for me, is that if there is a God or Goddess, I believe that these words refer more to energy and connection than to a personality, a figurehead. God or Goddess really is something we and the world create together. I use the term Goddess, rather than God, not because I see God as inherently gendered. The Venus of Willendorf is no more my idea of the image of God than the God of the Sistine Chapel. I say Goddess because it helps me to remember that it is not this image. It is still too easy to think I mean something different by God; it is too easy, when using that word, to slip into the same old immature version of God as the one who changes the outcomes of football games. What I experience that might be termed God or Goddess has come to me through symbols, images, connections that are traditionally termed feminine and are associated with feminist theology, like the labyrinth, like the image of the earth, or Gaia, like the web woven by Grandmother Spider.

What I know about prayer is that prayer isn't me talking, or me asking for things, or even for connection, to God. I've learned that prayer is about listening, at least for me. Further, it is about specifically listening for an understanding of my connection to the earth, to each of you, to society, and to all living things. It is also about listening for my vocation, my calling. What is it that I am meant to do? By which I don't mean, of course, that God will call me up and say, "Cindy, I want you to build me an ark. It should measure this many cubits wide by this many long, and this many deep." Rather, it is a way of knowing when I am on my path because I am in balance—what the Taoist might call in harmony with the Tao.

I've known this for a long time. I've been talking about what my spiritual model is for years.[7] One should be in right relationship first with oneself, knowing oneself and having integrity; secondly, to one's family and close circle of friends, neighbors, co-workers, etc.—love one's neighbor as oneself. Then, widening the circle, spirituality is to be in right relationship with society. Next, spirituality calls us to be in right relationship with the earth and its creatures, to walk lightly across her back. Finally, spirituality is to be in right relationship with the cosmos, or God. All along, I've known, abstractly, that I had this model.

But what I hadn't known, until these walks in the labyrinth, was that I wasn't living it. I wasn't living my spirituality—I was still living the spiritual practice I had been taught as a child. Preachers learn to preach their message, but sometimes we, or at least I, can forget to live it. It is easy to preach social justice, because I know I live it, at least to the best of my ability. It is harder to preach spirituality, because I haven't been living what I have known to be true. Each of us must find that balance, of knowing and doing, in order to be on our spiritual path. Perhaps I finally am.

Ancient Mother, I hear you calling. Ancient Mother, I hear your call.

The Paradox of Faith

December 14-15, 2002
The Gardner News

People are often very surprised when they find out that I'm a minister who doesn't believe in God. It is a seeming contradiction. "How can that be?" they ask me, "I don't understand." I am an agnostic, which means that I don't believe in God, but I don't disbelieve either, as an atheist would. My mind is not made up. In fact, I'm a true agnostic, because I believe it is impossible for me to know for sure at this time.

People often believe that this means I haven't been informed about religion, or that they should explain their own beliefs to me. While I'm always glad to hear about someone's experiences, and I celebrate their faith, I can assure you that after five years of theological school, and extensive reading of religious texts, one conversation is unlikely to change my mind.

Throughout my life, I've been confronted with the paradox of faith. How do you move from not believing to just believing, in the absence of proof. God is not something than one can have proof in—believing in God in a matter of faith. So how does one get faith? The answer is the paradox: One gets faith by simply having faith. Some have suggested to me that the way to believe in God is to first pray to God asking for faith. But prayer can't be genuine without faith. Until I muddle my way through the paradox, therefore, agnosticism is one answer.

There's a poetic beauty to this liminal, in-between state of theology. It leaves you open to experience, and not closed off to mystery, to wonder, or to truth.

Presumably, one might still be wondering—how can I be a minister who doesn't believe in God? The answer is simple. I'm a minister in a religion which welcomes every person's religious quest as valid and important, which believes in religious diversity, and which draws its beliefs and practices from all the world's religious traditions. Ministry, for me, is not about telling people what to believe, but about helping people along their religious paths, and supporting them on that journey.

Despite my agnosticism, I do have some strong beliefs about God. I know that if there is a God, that God is good. I know that God is loving. I know that God is larger than any of us can conceive. I believe God is larger than any one religious tradition and larger than any one text can describe.

How do I know these things? Again, it is the paradox of faith. I can't prove them to you any more than you could prove to me that I'm wrong. But I have a deep and abiding faith in them, and they make sense to me, as well.

There's a straight-forward logical argument that goes like this: God loves everyone, unconditionally. God is just, and all-powerful. God can save everyone, and wants to save everyone. Therefore, you are saved. I invite you to feel this possibility: God loves you so profoundly that he will not let you suffer eternally. God loves you so profoundly that her grace will ultimately enfold you and welcome you home.

The Name of God

January 18-19, 2003
The Gardner News

I'm very attached to my name. When I was growing up, I heard stories about how I was named. Ironically, I was named after a game show hostess. My parents, who are Southern, also wanted something which would sound Southern, so I was named "Cindy Leigh." My last name I can trace back for numerous generations, and I know it comes from the name of a location of a battle in Scotland, after which the area was called "the Bloody Hills of Lendrum." Even when I got married, I did not want to change my name. I know people who are very opinionated about what they are called. It matters deeply if they are called "Rob" instead of "Robert," or "Jen" instead of "Jenny." Our names are a deep and meaningful part of our identity.

Similarly, we are often very attached to our name for God. It often matters deeply to people what the name for God is, and what name we pray in, be it Jesus Christ, the Holy Spirit, Yahweh, Great Spirit, Jehovah, Brahman, Ultimate Reality, God, Goddess, Allah, the Ground of All Being, Father, Mother, or the Source of Life. Personally, when I pray, I use the term "Spirit of Life." Sometimes when someone leading a prayer uses a term that an individual person feels they can't relate to, they can get turned off, and lose the meaning of the message.

However, when someone addresses God by a different name, they are not speaking to only the God of their religion. They are not addressing a different God than yours, just because of a different name. If I say, "Great Spirit," I am not addressing the Native American God; if I pray to Jesus Christ I am praying to the Christian God, and if I call out to Allah, I am not calling out to the Muslim God. In all cases, I'm reaching out to the same God, I'm just using different languages or titles.

If someone calls me "Cindy," "Cyn," "Cynthia," "Landrum," "Rev.," "Professor," or even "hey you," I generally know when they are talking to me. God, even more so, is able to understand the complexity of believers, and the many languages and terms and prayer forms they use. William Shakespeare wrote, "What's in a name? That which we call a rose by any other name would smell as sweet." Similarly, Gertrude Stein wrote, "Rose is a rose is a rose is a rose." In other words, God by any name can hear your prayers, and God is God is God is God, no matter what you may call her.

In the Qur'an (or Koran), the scripture of the religion of Islam, there are ninety-nine names of Allah. They include: the Guide, the First, the Last, the Hidden, the Patient, the Eternal, the Creator, the Evolver, the Merciful, the Loving, the All-Forgiving, the Protecting Friend, and the Giver of Life. Jesus of Nazareth taught his followers, the Christians, to pray using a familiar family-oriented term for God: "Father."

In my own religion, we understand that people come to their religious understandings and beliefs in different ways. Some would say that there are many paths but one destination. Robert Frost's words about taking the road less traveled have always appealed to me. I know that there are conventional and tried-and-true ways to find religious insight, but for some of us we need to carve our own paths through the wilderness, and that can make "all the difference" in our success and peace and insight. For some, no term for God explains the mystery and wonder of the universe, and they use the language of science instead. I believe that if it is true that God is out there, that God can understand even this language for describing his creation.

So, while we can be attached to our own names for Gods, may we all remember to embrace the diversity of religion around us, and to know that each worshipper, no matter what their language or terminology, seeks the same things: peace, insight, closeness to God. You can even try using a different term in your own prayer. God will still hear you, love you, and walk with you on your path.

If There Is a God...

Winter 2009
The UU World

In considering the topics of Atheism, Agnosticism, Humanism, and the nature of God, it seems good to start with some general definitions. I capitalize here the terms Atheist, Agnostic, and Humanist out of a measure of respect for them as religious or secular systems. That is certainly arguable, and I imagine it will be argued. I support you who do not capitalize in your lack of capitals. I capitalize God except when I am specifically pointing out that there are a number of different gods that have been believed in by different cultures. It is important to recognize that Atheists don't believe in any god, however, not just the Judeo-Christian God.

Atheist: Someone who does not believe in God. There are many distinctions you can make among atheists—strong, weak, implicit, explicit, practical, theological—but the two major ones are strong atheism vs. weak atheism. A strong Atheist believes it is certain and clear that there is no God. A weak Atheist does not believe in God, but doesn't assert the lack of God.

Non-theist: Someone who does not assert a belief in God. I include Agnostics, Atheists, most Buddhists, and many others in this group. I generally reserve the term "Atheist" for individuals that are really strong Atheists, and use "non-theists" as the catch-all term.

Agnostic: Someone who does not know whether or not God exists. A weak Agnostic does not know if there is a God, but may feel they are still weighing evidence or will receive more evidence. A strong Agnostic believes it is ultimately unknowable whether or not God exists.

Humanist: I'll borrow a definition from the Continuum of Humanist Education: "Humanism is a godless philosophy based on reason and compassion." Secular Humanists assert that Humanism is a philosophy and has nothing to do with religion. Religious Humanists can see Humanism as a religion, albeit one that does not require a belief in God.

I put myself in the category of Agnostic and would call it a meta-strong Agnosticism: I believe we can't even know if the existence of God is the sort of thing that can be known. I am, personally, a Religious Humanist. I have preached a controversial sermon called "A Humanist's Search for God" and was told by some Humanists that a Humanist can't search for God. (I would call them church-going Secular Humanists, which seems like an oxymoron, yet I've encountered many in Unitarian Universalist churches.)

As an Agnostic, however, I have some very clear ideas of what kind of god is possible, and what kind is not. I have an absolute faith in this, and it is definitely a faith, because it is based on my passion, not on reason, if you want to make a distinction between faith and reason, although I reject such distinctions.

But my faith in what kind of god is impossible is not based in reason, although I'm sure that a reasonable argument for my atheism towards certain gods could be based in reason.

Here goes: If there is a God...

- God does not choose the victor in football games.
- God does not choose sides in human wars.
- God does not save some people from disease while letting others die.
- God does not "bless the United States of America" or any country.
- God does not send floods, hurricanes, or other natural disasters to punish people.
- God does not create diseases to punish people.
- God does not appear to some people and not others.
- God does not damn people for their sexual orientation or gender.
- God does not damn anyone.
- God does not demand belief in God.

I would say I am atheistic towards those gods, and, like all Atheism, in my opinion (here's the fighting words), this is based on a passionate belief that goes beyond reason. My heart and soul reject the idea that there could be a God who answers some people's prayers for life and health and not others', because I want to believe that if there is a God, God is good, and this would not match my definition of good.

I have heard people say that I do not pray or will not pray with people. This is not true. I do it all the time. I just don't do the "God, please heal so-and-so" type of prayer. When I am asked to pray for people, which I will do, I do not pray for God to heal them. I pray for them. I pray (which is to say, voice my hope, directed to a possible God) that they find the love or the strength or the compassion they need, in themselves and in their support networks. I voice what we are grateful for, or what our needs are. To me that is prayer. However, that is about as far as prayer can go, in my opinion. It can give voice to things, name things. That's about it. If you hear me give the prayer at a dinner at church, you'll hear something like, "Spirit of Life, we remember...(insert negative things that are relevant—poverty, hunger, etc.), and we are grateful for...(insert food, company, program, other noteworthy positive things). Blessed be and Amen." Pastoral prayers in situations like the hospital often take a similar structure.

Which brings me to the type of God I believe possible. I find it impossible to rule out the possibility of any sort of God. Yes, the world can be explained without God, but that doesn't prove the negation of the possibility, or the lack of possibility, that there is something more. The God I believe could be possible would be a God that, if God is a sentient being, cares for and loves all people equally and with a perfect love that, ultimately, saves everyone. More likely, God is something more like love, or positive energy, or the greater sum of all the parts of the universe, or something we create together in the work of love and justice. It is quite possible that humans do create God, and that God isn't fully created yet. Those kinds of God are possible, to me.

Where Do We Go From Here?

April 19, 2009
Universalist Unitarian Church of East Liberty
Clarklake, MI

This year the question posed to me for this year's "auction sermon" by a member of our congregation was, "Where do we go when we leave here?" ("Here" being Earth).

When I was an intern minister I was given this topic, as well. My internship supervisor did a Question Box sermon every year where he answered questions given to him by members of the congregation, and he saved one question for a sermon of its own, which he and I both preached our answer on. Here's what that church member wrote, many years ago:

> What do I do with the feeling of futility that comes from not believing in a life after death?...I have tried imagining my energy being absorbed into the universe at death, and that is the closest thing to comfort I can find. This still leaves me feeling like "Is this it?" If I don't think about it and just go about my daily life trying to live in the "now" it isn't so bad, but it still haunts me that everything I do that makes up my daily life and years is really all for nothing.

I was surprised as I looked over my response from nine years ago how much my own feelings had changed, deepened, and matured. Now, it seems, I have the chance to go back and answer this question again.

The first possibility, of course, is that people might go to a concrete afterlife, to Heaven or Hell, or to some place in-between, like purgatory. There are certainly a lot of people in our culture who believe this. Indeed, there are even some who claim to have experienced proof of it, such as in near-death experiences. There are also scientists who have studied near-death experiences and who believe profoundly in the results they've accumulated.

Like our Universalist ancestors, I reject outright the concept of Hell. The Universalists were called the "no Hell" religion. They followed a logical—yes logical—approach to their understanding of God, which said that a loving God is not a God of hellfire, of brimstone, of damnation. Ultimately, they believed, every soul could be reconciled with God; every soul would go to Heaven. As someone raised Unitarian Universalist, I was raised with this sort of Universalist belief, although I also absorbed the larger cultural belief in Hell, as well. It was partly a Universalist reaction to the concept of a loving God damning souls to eternal Hell that originally broke down my belief in God. When I later rediscovered Universalism, though, I did not regain my belief in God. Faith, once lost, is not easily regained.

But, all the same, I do not believe a literal sort of Heaven is a likely scenario. This is not to reject the profound experiences of people who have had near-death experiences, but to say that, for me, there is no reason based on the evidence, to conclude that this is what happens. I know a lot of people don't believe Heaven is literally flying around in flowing white gowns with harps and angel's wings. I think the accepted definition would be a state of extreme happiness and perfection, completed by a closeness to God—another dimension in which an experience of wholeness, completion, and peace abounds.

That sounds really wonderful. Certainly, I can understand the longing for it. For those of us who have had a belief in Heaven, and then lost Heaven, it can be very difficult. It can be depressing. To have God and then lose God, to have the promise of Heaven, and then lose the promise of Heaven, is a loss that may be mourned, for it is a painful loss.

Another popular religious view is that of reincarnation. Just as many religions, such as Judaism, Christianity, Islam, and others, have heavens, or both heavens and hells, many religions have a belief in reincarnation. For Buddhism and Hinduism in particular, reincarnation is very much a part of their systems of belief.

There are people who have studied reincarnation who believe it to be a scientific fact, although certainly not conclusively enough that it is unanimously accepted by the scientific community. I found it interesting that Jim Tucker, the author of *Life Before Life: Children's Memories of Previous Lives*, does not conclude that everyone necessarily reincarnates, even though he believes some people do. He suggests that one possibility for reincarnation is that it may be similar to how many people understand ghosts happen—that many people pass on directly to the afterlife, while some people with particularly traumatic deaths may linger as ghosts or may reincarnate into another body.

Speaking of ghosts, becoming ghosts is another option for where we go from here. Many who believe in ghosts don't believe that everyone becomes a ghost—that ghosts are spirits who are not at rest for one reason or another. However, there are also religions that believe all of the ancestors essentially become spirits that are still present in this world. Take, for example, the concept of Kami in the Shinto faith, where every living and non-living thing has a kami, or spirit, or beliefs of some Native American about ancestor spirits.

All these options—Heaven, Hell, reincarnation, ghosts—rely on a concept of a soul or spirit, and the idea that something that is us goes on after our body stops. The alternative to this belief is the belief that our spirit is not something separate from body, not something beyond nature, but really just that which we might call personality or even energy. In this view, when our bodies stop, the spirit stops. Many Humanist Unitarian Universalists share this belief—that what happens when we die is that we die: end of story for our spirit, for anything that can be called us. What happens then is that we decompose—and decomposing means a lack of composition. It means a lack of anything that can still be called "me." We are literally dust to dust, ashes to ashes. If we are lucky enough to be buried in such a way that we can become one with the earth, we become one with the earth. Whether we are literally scattered like ashes or not, we might as well be, for there is no person there remaining. The person lives on only so much as they live on in memory, which means, for most of humanity, within a few generations we are mostly forgotten. We can live on in the ways our lives impacted the world, the works we created, the lives we created, the ways large and small we impacted our environments, but who we are, as people, that individual personality with its humor, its quirks, its likes and dislikes, that is gone.

My mind tells me that this is the most logical of outcomes. This seems most probable, most logical. Logically, it is the description of what scientifically happens after death. It is quite possible that this is all there is, that there is no greater glory. This is what I believed at the start of my ministry, years ago, when I examined this question. I wrote:

> I do believe that everything comes to an end, and mourning those ends is a part of the deal we get when we live. Loss is the price of being connected to people. It is worth it. When facing our own death, it may not be okay for us, but the joy is that we lived, and we loved, and we made the world a better place for having been there. What makes this less depressing, what makes all of this even glorious, is that I truly believe there is a "Kingdom of God" coming—as in when, in the "Lord's Prayer," we say, "thy kingdom come, thy will be done." The Kingdom of God is not an afterlife. It is not somewhere we go when we die; it is about hope and courage. It is something we are creating, and striving towards, in every generation, here on earth. I think we are getting closer to it. So even if you and I will not be remembered directly, we will have moved the earth as a whole, even the cosmos, towards creating a Kingdom of God.

That's where I was then. But I find now that my mind rejects this idea of finitude just as much as my mind has trouble grasping the infinite. I have always found it impossible to fathom infinity, even when just reduced to numbers, to fathom that numbers always go on—that there is always one more and one more and one more. But just as unfathomable is the idea of finitude, when trying to apply it to myself— that like the wound clock that just stops, one day I will be thinking and breathing and living and loving, and one day there will be no more me here anymore. My mind stops, rejects, balks at that notion. Perhaps this is due to simply growing older, and as we grow closer to death it becomes more real, and the ability I had to live purely in the world of what was logical, what was scientific, has been tempered by the increasing reality of death as I lose more people I have known and cared for.

I find that I am not really willing to give up on the idea of that greater glory, that completeness, that wholeness, that peace just yet. I'm not a believer in Heaven or reincarnation, or becoming a ghost, but I do really think there is a soul, something that is me that is more than just this body. I also think that just as every atom becomes something else, all the atoms that were me continue after my death, so, too, this soul continues in some fashion, as well. I would call this, "becoming one with the universe." What does that mean exactly? Well, I'm still the true agnostic. I don't know for certain what is true. In this case, I don't even know what the thing I might believe looks like. That's about as vague as one can get. What I have said before is that nothing that you are is lost forever, by which I mean that just as the atoms you are comprised of—the oxygen, the hydrogen—continue on, that spark of you continues on in some way, too. That may not mean consciousness, exactly, for I don't believe we are spirits looking down at the world, but rather that we are joined together in a larger form somehow. Perhaps that is God. Perhaps that's completeness. That's where I come to, when I explore my own beliefs about God and eternity and death.

The wonderful thing about Unitarian Universalism is that we can, individually, believe any, none, or even all of these ideas. Because whichever of these is true, in some great sense it doesn't matter. For I truly believe that what does matter is the here and the now—this world, this earth, and this life. What will come will come, and come what may, our calling remains the same. Our job is to live the best possible lives we can, to strive to build that kingdom of God on earth, because if there is a heaven, it will get us there. If there is karma and reincarnation, it will move us up the great wheel of Samsara, and if this is all there is, well, we will have made this world and this life the best possible for now. Our faith is a this-worldly faith. We are about creating that vision here, on earth, as soon as possible. We are not about waiting until we die for the reward to be handed to us, but about working for it to happen here, on this world, for everyone's sake. We are about pushing, pulling, moving the world to be better than it is. This, the here and now, is not all there is. There is a greater glory, and you and I are building it every day.

Extremists for Love

February 13, 2010
Universalist Unitarian Church of East Liberty
Clarklake, MI

In our church, we have written on our altar "God is Love." That's a pretty ordinary statement. It is found in all sorts of churches. Yet it is seldom really lived out in its fullest understanding of what it means and what it implies we are to do in response to this statement.

Our Unitarian Universalist Association president, Peter Morales, said in a Valentine's Day letter:

> To be a person of faith is to stand on the side of love. We are especially called to love those who are despised, powerless and marginalized. This sacred love is not just an emotion. Love acts. Love cares for those in need. Love demands that we take a stand. Love requires us to stand with those whom others reject and vilify.[8]

What does love demand of us? A lot of churches would follow up a statement like "God is love" with one like, "Hate the sin, love the sinner." This is not what we mean by love in the Universalist tradition.

Across our country this weekend, over 100 Unitarian Universalist churches are taking part in something called "Reimagining Valentine's Day," hosted by the Standing on the Side of Love campaign. Standing on the Side of Love, or "sizzle" as SSL is called, is a new Unitarian Universalist campaign to encourage people to stand on the side of love against identity-based oppressions. The primarily focus of SSL is on two types of identity-based groups that frequently experience oppression: lesbian, gay, bisexual and transgender people, and immigrants. But what we as a movement are about, when we say we're "Standing on the Side of Love" is something much bigger than that.

Back in the fall, I was at a meeting of MOSES, a Detroit-area group of religious leaders, and we were talking about healthcare reform. One of the pastors there said that when he's asked what side he is on in issues like this, he says he's on the side of the suffering. We're saying something similar with our campaign. We're saying we're on the side of Love, and since we say "God is Love" up here on our altar, we're saying by extension that we will stand on the side of God.

On the other side, over and over again in our society, I hear religious groups letting themselves be the voices of hate and oppression. I also hear the new atheists saying that this is all religion is, that religion by its very nature is exclusive, defining who is in and who is out, and that religion is, by its nature, hateful, defining who are the chosen people and the recipients of God's love, and who are not.

Our religion, by nature of our Universalist heritage, defies all that. We come from a people who understood God not by the limits, but by the expansiveness, of God's love. Universalism is what enabled us to become the religion that we are today—by its very nature accepting that love, universal love, is at the ground of all being, and by believing that that love encompasses people across religious boundaries, across boundaries of race and class, across boundaries of sexual orientation, across boundaries of country of origin. We are a faith that understood from its earliest years the expansiveness of God's love.

The metaphor for God of a parent, of a father, is used so often in Christianity, yet we never take it to its logical conclusion of love. In our larger society, we hear the prodigal son story, where the son is welcomed home by the father with welcome arms, yet that very message of welcome and acceptance is denied by many. However, here, in our house of worship, we know that when we say "God is love, love never faileth," that that God is a verb—God is love—the love that we show each other, the love that we show the stranger, the love that is the true message of religion.

Let me share what others are saying across this country this week.

My colleague Cecilia Kingman in Wenatchee, Oregon, said this week, "As for us, though, we proclaim God's love for all people—that great, redeeming love which has no limit. And we invite everyone who places compassion, justice and love at the center of your faith to join us in standing on the side of love."[9] In Potsdam, New York, an organizer, Austin Kenyon said, "This weekend is a symbol, it's done purposefully, to reimagine Valentine's Day as a holiday. To reimagine it not as just a holiday of candy and Hallmark cards. But as a day of love and acceptance for everyone."[10] In Maryland, on the Beltway, the Rev. Diane Teichert said that she would no longer sign marriage licenses, saying, "Valentine's Day is about more than romance and chocolates...It's about the transforming power of love in our lives."[11]

In Ogden, Utah, the minister Rev. Theresa Novak said this week, "We understand love to be a verb, an act that transcends fear and extends beyond individuals to embrace a community."[12] In Redwood City, California, the Rev. Sean Dennison said, "I believe that every major religion has compassion and love at its center. The message of love may get lost or warped, or co-opted by power, but at its heart, staying true to our religious values means standing on the side of Love—not only romantic love, but love that demands fairness, equity, compassion, and justice for all."[13] In Minnesota, the Rev. Meg Riley said:

I love all of the ripples that spread out over the waters from this one event. Ripples which extend out to hold a wide variety of religious people, who share the same conviction about marriage equality....

In such moments, when we experience being one people, I feel that I am living my religious mission. We all know that the forces of hate and fear are strong. Here's our chance to know that the force of love, when we stand on the side of love, is even stronger.[14]

In Boston, our Unitarian Universalist Association president said:

This Valentine's Day has been proclaimed Standing on the Side of Love Day. People of many faiths across America are worshipping, meeting, and taking action to stand with those who most need our love and compassion today.... This Valentine's Day, as we cherish those closest to us and as we celebrate the divine gift of love, let us dare to embrace a larger love. Join with thousands across America who are standing on the side of love for all people.[15]

If there's one thing that we're about, folks, as Unitarian Universalists, this is it. We are the people who see that love is the center of religious life, and we choose to live our religion through embodying love in this world.

The Rev. Martin Luther King, Jr. said in his letter from the Birmingham Jail:

Was not Jesus an extremist for love: "Love your enemies, bless them that curse you, do good to them that hate you, and pray for them which despitefully use you, and persecute you." Was not Amos an extremist for justice: "Let justice roll down like waters and righteousness like an ever-flowing stream." Was not Paul an extremist: "I bear in my body the marks of the Lord Jesus." Was not Martin Luther an extremist? "Here I stand; I cannot do otherwise, so help me God." And John Bunyan: "I will stay in jail to the end of my days before I make a butchery of my conscience." And Abraham Lincoln: "This nation cannot survive half slave and half free." And Thomas Jefferson: "We hold these truths to be self evident, that all men are created equal..." So the question is not whether we will be extremists, but what kind of extremists we will be. Will we be extremists for hate or for love? Will we be extremists for the preservation of injustice, or for the extension of justice?

Let us, brothers and sisters of the Universalist Unitarian Church of East Liberty, be extremists for love. Let us stand in the name of love, let us sing in the name of love, let us dance in the name of love, let us worship in the name of love, let us *live* in the name of love, and let us be extremists in our loving.

May it be so.

Responding with Love

August 10, 2008
Jackson Citizen Patriot

Most people have heard about the shootings that occurred July 27th in the Tennessee Valley Unitarian Universalist Congregation in Knoxville, Tenn. Two people were killed and seven others were wounded when a man began shooting during an intergenerational Sunday service featuring a production of "Annie."

People responded immediately with shock, grief and anger. That was news.

But what people often don't hear about is what happens afterward—the small gestures, the work of a church community to pull itself together, the reaching out of the larger community. The responses as time goes on are of healing, love and hope. These things are not news. But they are important pieces of our lives as we respond to tragedy.

The day after the tragedy, members of the Tennessee Valley congregation gathered at the nearby Presbyterian church for a vigil. The children and adults, who only a day before witnessed horror and tragedy, sang out the words from Annie's "Tomorrow." While surely they were still experiencing shock, anger, denial and grief, they raised their voices in a song about hope.

The Knoxville congregation members couldn't know it yet, but that night they were joined by churches across the nation in vigils. That same Monday evening, voices were being raised in prayer and song in our congregation here and in at least 50 other Unitarian Universalist congregations across the nation.

By the middle of that week, more than 200 vigils would be scheduled. That is an amazing outpouring of love from a denomination with little more than 1,000 congregations.

A few years ago, the world watched in awe as the Amish people responded to a shooting in one of their schoolhouses. The Amish taught the world about their faith as they responded with love and forgiveness. Today, we learn about a very different faith community, but again the response is love and forgiveness.

William Sinkford, president of the Unitarian Universalist Association of Congregations, was asked if he believed the shooter was going to Hell. He responded, "In my religious tradition, we would say that that person had been living in a hell here on earth, for years."[16]

We first heard that the shooting was born out of hate—hatred for liberals, hatred aimed at a Unitarian Universalist congregation for its open acceptance of gays and lesbians, and its work against oppression and discrimination—and later learned there were other possible motives. We may never understand Adkisson's true motivations. What we can understand is this: Had Jim Adkisson entered the doors of the church in peace, asking for help, he would have found a wonderful community willing to offer love and support.

The Tennessee Valley congregation did not let hatred and anger and tragedy be the last word. Its message of hope, acceptance and universal love will be heard louder than ever, just as in the song: "The sun'll come out/ Tomorrow/ Bet your bottom dollar/ That tomorrow/ There'll be sun!"

To not Live and Die in Vain

April 30, 2006
Universalist Unitarian Church of East Liberty
Clarklake, MI

The president of our church board asked me to write on this subject: "We don't want those who have lost their lives (for various reasons: war, natural disaster, murder, etc.) to have died in vain. What are the criteria to determine whether or not someone has died in vain? If no one has ever died in vain, then why do we even make the statement? Is it possible someone could die in vain?" These are great questions-and very difficult ones.

I was speaking with my good friend who is an oncologist, and she sees a lot of deaths—people who die from cancer all the time. Is that meaningful, she asks? Aren't all these deaths "in vain," to some extent? Does a person *not* die in vain just because that person's family then goes and starts a foundation for breast cancer research? Deaths can be seen as senseless, meaningless tragedies all the time.

A very literal understanding of the concept of dying in vain would say that if someone specifically chose to die so that some cause or purpose could be fulfilled, and yet for whatever reason that cause wasn't fulfilled, then that person died in vain. People often take that concept and broaden it to any tragic death, to say that if we don't do x, y, or z, then the tragic death would be in vain.

At a time when our country is at war, this is particularly in people's minds; in vigils around the country, people read the names of the dead, and mourn them. Very often we hear the statement that if we don't fight this war to its conclusion, and win this war, then the soldiers have all died in vain. Others use the same appeal, to avoid deaths in vain, to support quite a different stance—immediately ending the war. One way they do this is to say that all deaths in war are deaths in vain, so we need to stop the war to stop more people from dying in vain. Others reason that if their child's death motivates them to stop the war, then their child will not have died in vain. Our differing understandings of how we ascribe meaning to lives and deaths come into conflict as we deal with this war in particular.

There is, as I said, the sort of literal understanding, the matter-of-fact answer to, "what does it mean to die in vain?" But I want to explore this from a few deeper levels. The first is from a psychological perspective, from theories of moral development.

Carol Gilligan, in her book *In a Different Voice*, talks about gender differences in moral reasoning, which I think is valuable here. She took Lawrence Kohlberg's steps of moral reasoning and explained why women, as a group, seemed to score lower—it was because they were using a different paradigm entirely. Their moral reasoning was more relational, and sometimes outside the box, if the box was defined by Kohlberg. The classic moral question is the Heinz dilemma. In the Heinz dilemma, the subjects are asked what they would do if their spouse was dying and they couldn't afford medicine: Would they follow the law and let their spouse die, which is one type of moral reasoning, or, following another type of moral reasoning, would they rob the pharmacy to save their spouse? When asked this, women would try to step outside the box and talk about negotiating deals with the pharmacist or organizing a fundraising event. Their answers were stuck at Kohlberg's stage three, because their ideas of right and wrong were not based on higher moral authorities like God, on a relationship-based morality. Rather than caught between moral law and civil law, the women were caught between selfishness and altruism.

I bring this up because when you use this type of moral reasoning, the question of dying in vain gets yet another turn. When talking to a friend about the subject of dying in vain, she asked, well when does someone *not* die in vain? (Again, believing that all deaths are in vain.) When I said that some people might define it as a case in which someone specifically chooses to die to fulfill a certain cause, and the cause is triumphant, she said, "Well, but what if there was another way, and they didn't have to die? Then didn't they die in vain?" Her favorite examples are from the television show *24*—in one episode the hero of the show has to fly a plane to let a bomb explode over a place where it can't hurt anyone, but he'll die in the process. However, in this show he doesn't die, and the bomb doesn't explode—the third way is always found.

The truth is, maybe another way can always be found. Maybe there is always a way that we can choose life, not death, and that all deaths, therefore, are in vain. A summary of Gilligan's third level of moral reasoning, the morality of nonviolence, states, "At this third level, women have largely rejected the notion of moral self-sacrifice as immoral in its power to hurt the self. The principle of nonviolence—an injunction against hurting—becomes the basic premise underlying all moral judgments. Looking after the welfare of people is now a self-chosen and *universal* obligation that permits the woman to recognize a moral equality between herself and others that must be considered when making moral judgments."[17] Using this framework, the moral logic that tells people that they should die in a way that is about moral self-sacrifice—the kind of death that we talk about *not* being in vain, in the sense that a hero dying for a cause is a noble death not in vain—this type of death can be considered by some to be against the moral value of nonviolence.

The next perspective that I want to consider is the perspective of Eastern religions, particularly Buddhism. The deaths we're talking about when we talk about dying in vain are young deaths, out-of-time deaths, out of the normal pattern of life that we all assume will be ours: to grow old, to die before our children do and after our parents do. We sometimes hear the phrase "senseless tragedy," and it is somewhat equivalent to the concept of dying in vain: the idea that a death has no meaning—senseless—or that its purpose was not fulfilled.

There is a story about the Buddha that speaks to this type of death. A young woman comes to the Buddha, carrying her dead child in her arms, seeking to understand death, and her own suffering at the loss of her child. The Buddha tells her to go to the village, and to bring him some rice from a house that has not known death. She searches the village, going to every door, and eventually returns, empty handed, as of course everyone has known death. Through this she understands that suffering and death touch everyone, and cannot be avoided.[18]

I am not a Buddhist. I do not believe that suffering is the universal experience to focus one's religion around. I have a more optimistic existentialism. However, I do agree with Buddhism that death and suffering are universal, and from this I take an understanding that death, in and of itself, is meaningless. As Mary Oliver puts it, "Don't we all die at last, and too soon?" But here's the difference of my optimistic existentialism: *We are the meaning makers.*

This brings me to my third perspective on this question: the optimistic existentialist perspective.

I want to begin by saying that I don't believe anyone ever *lives* in vain. Every life has meaning and purpose. Our Universalist heritage teaches us this by saying that every person is saved. The reason that every person is saved is because, essentially, every person is worth saving. Every person, in the language of the Unitarian Universalist principles, has inherent worth and dignity. Therefore, every *person* has meaning and purpose. Every life is itself full of meaning, full of potential for good and for harm, full of ideas, and full of the potential for love.

I begin with life, because I think this is part of the answer. If nobody lives in vain, then there is one sense in which nobody dies in vain—nobody's life is without meaning, and no death is without meaning. These questions about living and dying in vain are in large part a question about meaning. What is the meaning to life, to death? In his book *Man's Search for Meaning*, Holocaust survivor Viktor Frankl states, "The meaning of life differs from man to man, from day to day and from hour to hour. What matters, therefore, is not the meaning of life in general but rather the specific meaning of a person's life at a given moment. To put the question in general terms would be comparable to the question posed to a chess champion:

'Tell me, Master, what is the best move in the world?' There simply is no such thing as the best or even a good move apart from a particular situation in a game and the particular personality of one's opponent. The same holds for human existence." Frankl further explains that in the concentration camps:

> We had to learn ourselves and, furthermore, we had to teach the despairing men, that *it did not really matter what we expected from life, but rather what life expected from us.* We needed to stop asking about the meaning of life, and instead to think of ourselves as those who were being questioned by life—daily and hourly. Our answer must consist, not in talk and meditation, but in right action and in right conduct. Life ultimately means taking the responsibility to find the right answer to its problems and to fulfill the tasks which it constantly sets for each individual.

Frankl says that every person's meaning in life is different, and that the meaning is taken from each person's unique and special destiny.

Frankl also gives an example of a young woman in the concentration camp who was dying, and who knew that she would die in the next few days. He writes:

> Pointing through the window of the hut, she said, "This tree here is the only friend I have in my loneliness." Through that window she could see just one branch of a chestnut tree, and on that branch were two blossoms. "I often talk to this tree," she said to me.... I asked her if the tree replied. "Yes." What did it say to her? She answered, "It said to me, 'I am here—I am here—I am life, eternal life.'"[19]

Frankl's story shows a woman facing death, and still, in the concentration camp, dying as she is, still living through that tree. This is living, not dying.

In his curriculum for adult religious education, *Building Your Own Theology*, the Rev. Richard S. Gilbert says, "We are the meaning makers." Paraphrasing Albert Camus, he says, "There is no inherent meaning embedded in the universe. Human beings don't *find* meaning—we *create* it out of the raw stuff of our own experience. So, if the cosmos, history, and life have no meaning to discover, we can live so that our lives have meaning. We are its originators. We behold the stars and write our meanings in them."[20]

I believe as we live, so too do we die. We are the meaning makers. If a death has meaning, it is because we, the living, have given it such. If we take that idea seriously, that we are the meaning makers, then maybe the answer to "Can we die in vain?" is actually no. If someone, after a death, finds meaning in it, then the death had meaning, and was not in vain.

What does that mean, "We are the meaning makers?" It means that we have a religious responsibility to make sure that no one around us dies in vain. Therefore, I would define dying in vain as death without subsequent reflection by the living on that death, without impact on the living, without legacy. For me, living and dying in vain is not about "mission completed." We all die with things we would have liked to have done. Sometimes people die for a cause unfulfilled (or even a wrong cause). But this, I do not believe, means dying in vain.

In a Unitarian Universalist memorial service, ministers in our faith are trained to do something a little different than ministers do in other, particularly Christian, traditions. In many Christian funeral or memorial services, you will hear the minister talk about salvation, about Heaven, about eternal rewards for a life of faith. Their words identify that in some sense a life was in vain, and the death was a senseless tragedy, if the deceased did not get to Heaven and was not a faithful follower of the limited creed which denies universal salvation. For those who see in the resurrection the potential for salvation, Jesus Christ is the ultimate example of the concept that some deaths are in vain and others are not. "He died for your sins," as they say—therefore his death has the most meaning possible.

Our Unitarian Universalist faith handles things differently. A fundamental part of our Universalist heritage is the belief in universal salvation. This creed, for those who embrace it, says that every person goes to Heaven. In this faith, how can any death be in vain, if we all have eternal glory? I believe Jesus' death, for example, wasn't necessary for our salvation. God can find a way to save us all without a sacrificial lamb, without requiring the blood of others to be shed for ours. From universal salvation, I reach the conclusion that all death has meaning.

As our faith also carries a more existentialist Humanism, however, there are many who would say every person dies the same: We all go back into the earth, we all rot away. Therefore, how is any death anything other than just death?

But for both Humanist and Universalist, since our fate, whatever it is, is universal, we do the same thing in a memorial service: We talk about the person who has died. We pull together the stories, the photos, the memories, the mementos, the hymns, and the readings that reflect the person's values and the sayings they said, and we remember them. It is a profoundly different approach to talk about humanity, not about theology, and to talk about the person that was, and that person's impact on the living, rather than simply quote scripture and interpret it.

What this means to me is that in our tradition no one dies in vain, because we, the meaning makers, give each life meaning. In the true existentialist sense, life and death—existence itself—is meaningless. We provide the meaning, the essence, during and after the fact.

Meaning is for the living, in the living. Thoreau tells us to live deliberately, to suck all the marrow out of life, and to not, when we come to die, discover that we had not lived. Thoreau tells us that it is living itself that makes us not die in vain. Mary Oliver writes, "Going to Walden is not so easy a thing as a green visit. It is the slow and difficult trick of living, and finding it where you are." There, I believe, I find my final answer to the question of whether or not we die in vain and what the meaning of life is: meaningfulness is not easy; it is found in the slow and difficult path that is living, it is found where we are, every day. We are not meant for a hero's death. We are meant to pour our lives into our loves, and then our deaths, through our relationships to those we love, will not be in vain.

Vocation

April 15, 2007
Universalist Unitarian Church of East Liberty
Clarklake, MI

Today's sermon comes from a member of the congregation's question: "Many of us work in jobs, but how often does that work become a vocation? Any work, including church work, can be a vocation if we but make it so. We all want to be part of something larger than ourselves. How can we share in the work of the church so that the work has meaning, and it becomes vocation rather than work?"

I begin with the story of Jonah. How many of us can recall it? Here's my retelling, in brief. Jonah was called—by God. God tells Jonah to go to Nineveh and preach to the people there. Jonah flees from this calling—he goes the other way. Of course, there is no escaping God, and the boat Jonah is on is set upon by fierce storms. Finally, Jonah confesses to the crew that it is he who has angered God. He tells them to cast him overboard, which they do. Then, finally, Jonah is swallowed by the whale. And in the belly of that whale he prays to God, who eventually frees him from the whale. Once freed, Jonah does go to Nineveh, and he preaches about his experience, and the people hear it and turn away from their wicked ways.

The word "vocation" comes from vocare—voice, or calling. For many people, this calling is a very literal experience, like it was for Jonah. For others, like myself, it is more metaphor. But whichever way you sense your calling, calling can be a difficult thing to heed. We all know stories of people who do something with their life—a job, work, something to pay the bills—and then realize that they *have to*, feel *compelled to* give it up to do what they are called to do—be it ministry, be it art, be it teaching, be it something connected to the earth, to justice, to people. For many people, heeding the call means spending time in the belly of the whale—it is a risk, it is scary, it is dark and lonely, and ultimately, it is something you do because you have to. When I was entering ministry, I heard it time and again from colleagues: Don't go into ministry unless you *have to*. They didn't mean that because it is a bad job—it isn't—they meant that because it is not a job, it is a vocation, an identity, and a calling.

The poet William Safford, in a poem titled, "Ask Me," writes, "Some time when the river is ice ask me mistakes I have made. Ask me whether what I have done is my life." Author and educator Parker Palmer uses these lines in opening his book *Let Your Life Speak*. The title comes from an old Quaker saying. Palmer says "let your life speak" doesn't means to live up to our highest ideals, but rather: "Before you tell your life what you intend to do with it, listen for what it intends to do with you. Before you tell your life what truths and values you have decided to live up to, let your life tell you what truths you embody, what values you represent."[21] From this perspective, letting your life speak, letting your life become vocation, doesn't involve doing what you think God means for you to do, like Jonah. It means listening to that still, small voice *within*. It means following the soul. In the language of Rabbi Zusya, in a Hasidic tale, it means: "In the coming world, they will not ask me: 'Why were you not Moses?' They will ask me: 'Why were you not Zusya?'"[22] Vocation is Zusya being Zusya, me being the most me I can be, you being the most you that you can be.

Classically, the word "vocation" means a religious calling to professional religious leadership or, even more specifically, to the priesthood or monastery. Of course we define it more broadly now to mean any profession or job where we are heeding that higher calling or deeper calling. From what I've observed in Unitarian Universalist circles, we have a lot of people who know something about calling. I've asked Unitarian Universalist congregations for a show of hands on how many of them are in social work, in a medical profession, in a profession related to connecting with the earth or the cosmos, in a teaching profession, in justice work, or in a non-profit or NGO. When we look around, most of the hands are up. These jobs are easy to see as vocations. If you add in others who see their jobs as vocations, you have almost all Unitarian Universalists.

We are people who often choose work that connects us to our values. Our pews are full of people with vocation. Of course, I know this doesn't apply to everyone. Sometimes we can be frustrated in a job that doesn't allow us to find our sense of calling within it. On the other hand, sometimes we can enjoy a job very much that we don't consider a calling, but which can feed the spirit if not the soul, and be great for our energy and for our families. Just keep in mind that everyone can sometimes end up in the belly of the whale. If that happens to you, connect back to some of the people in the Unitarian Universalist faith—you may know some people who know what it is to be in the belly of the whale, and who can offer you a candle in that darkness.

I don't think that every job has to be a vocation, or that we can always find in every task that sense of calling. While I have a sense of calling in my profession, there are certainly tasks that I perform not because of that calling, but because they just need to be done—for example, going through all the mail. It stacks up on my desk—all those newsletters from other churches, and catalogs from church supply companies, and flyers from every non-profit in town. I don't find a sense of calling in reading through all this mail, or in photocopying readings for an adult RE class, or in filing my sermons, or in a lot of the other "administrivia" that goes hand-in-hand with the job of ministry. (By the way, there's a reason that the word clerical is shared by clergy and by secretarial workers alike—much of the ministry is administrative work, although much of it goes unseen.)

Similarly, I know there are numerous volunteers for churches and they probably don't enjoy every little thing that they do, but they do them anyway. Not every piece of the work—like committee meetings and dealing with difficult clients or colleagues—will feel like part of the calling. Yet we must do it all, anyway. We're lucky, really, if we can see the vocation in the larger picture of the work we do. It is in a lot of way a luxury—not of money, or of velvets, but a luxury of the soul that many don't have. Yet it is also hard work for the soul, too, to be engaged in the work of vocation. The calling doesn't always call us to where we want to go—sometimes we have to go to Nineveh, whether we like it or not.

How do you make your existing work a vocation, or the work you do for an agency such as a church a calling, a ministry? To answer that, I have a story from *One Hundred Wisdom Stories Around the World.* The story tells of a young man who sets off to travel the world and seek his fortune, as so many in the old tales do. He travels through many lands—some happy, some sad, some peaceful, some warlike. He then eventually comes to that mythical cottage on the road. It is a little shop, with a kind old shopkeeper. The shopkeeper asks him what he wants, telling him they have everything one could want. Tired after his journey, weary from the road and all the sorrow he has seen, he responds:

> "I want peace—in my own family, in my native land and in the whole world...I want to make something good of my life...I want those who are sick to be well again and those who are lonely to have friends...I want those who are hungry to have enough to eat...I want every child born on this planet today to have a chance to be educated...I want everyone on earth to live in freedom...I want this world to be a kingdom of love..."
> Gently, the shopkeeper broke in. "I'm sorry," came the quiet reply. "I should have explained. We don't supply the fruits here. We only supply the seeds."[23]

How do you make of your work a vocation? How do you feel like you're part of something larger than yourself? How does the work you do in volunteering for the larger faith become more than just work and become a ministry? We can supply the seeds in Unitarian Universalism. The seeds are a place of freedom, a house of peace, a community of earnest and caring souls. The seeds are opportunity for genuine service and opportunity for spiritual growth. But you must grow the fruits.

In terms of growing work into ministry, it means taking the opportunity to find a mentor to teach you a new skill, or to mentor someone else using a skill you already have. It means, as a colleague of mine once said, when you disagree with what is said from the pulpit, next week you sit a little closer—because you value our freedom of belief and freedom of dissent.

Growing the fruits means that you have to work: plant, water, feed, tend, weed, and—most of all—wait. Whether the transformation happens in the belly of the whale or slowly like a fruit ripening on a vine, transformation is a process that begins within, opening your heart, preparing a place.

In religious community, we work to prepare the place, to open the heart, to plant the seed, so that transformation may begin. Our job is to create a religious space where one can find vocation, find the quest, get on the path. We don't supply the answers, we supply the fertile soil, and maybe some rain. The rest is up to you. May you find your vocation, your heart's path, and the religious community to be with you on your journey.

May it be so.

So It Goes: A Tribute to Kurt Vonnegut, Jr.

May 6, 2007
Universalist Unitarian Church of East Liberty
Clarklake, MI

Many may be wondering why I chose to preach on Kurt Vonnegut, Jr., aside the desire to commemmorate a celebrated author's death. Indeed, I am wondering this myself. I wasn't necessarily going to preach on Vonnegut, and when I decided to do so, a series of coincidences started hitting me. For example, members of my church, I found out, had written songs about him that we could share in the service. Then I was reading a favorite book of poetry in preparation for a workshop I was doing at a local retreat center—Anne Sexton's *Transformations*—only to discover that Vonnegut had written the introduction. I had also found myself thinking of the phrase "Dulce et decorum est pro patria mori" ("It is sweet and right to die for your country"), used in Wilfred Owen's World War I poem, for some reason the words floating through my mind, only to find that Vonnegut, too, had referenced the old phrase. So, Vonnegut it is. I was clearly supposed to preach on him.

He's a contrary figure—an anti-authoritarian author of works celebrated and decried. His works are taught by some, and burned by others—a fact I think he found somewhat humorous. He writes about the most profound and sublime, and yet also the most crass and mundane aspects of life. His works are filled with swearwords and sex, sex, and more sex—and I think he never wrote a credible female character in his life. Yet he is celebrated for the politics of his books, as well as for the artistry of them.

And, yes, Vonnegut can be considered a Unitarian Universalist. Well, at least he said, "I am an atheist (or at best a Unitarian who winds up in church quite a lot)."[24] But he also had other Unitarian Universalist credentials, other than this sort of sideways admission of being in our ranks. For one, his grandparents were members of the Unitarian Universalist church in Indianapolis.[25] More notably, however, Vonnegut spoke at the First Parish Unitarian Church in Cambridge, Massachusetts, on the 200th anniversary of the birth of William Ellery Channing. Channing was the author of the sermon "Unitarian Christianity" that in many ways defined Unitarianism and set our movement going. At that event, in true Unitarian style, Vonnegut tells of a passion play he had begun to write for his daughter, who had become a trinitarian. In it, a rich Roman man says to those holding vigil at the crucifixion, "My goodness! The way you are worshipping him, you would think he was the Son of your God." A person, perhaps, he says, Mary Magdalene, responds for the group at the cross, "Oh no, sir. If he were the Son of our God, he would not need us. It is because he is a common human being exactly like us that we are here—doing, as common people must, what little we can."[26] His passion play is pure Unitarianism.

Another speech Kurt Vonnegut, Jr., gave was at the Ware Lecture in 1986. The Ware Lecture is the cornerstone lecture of our Unitarian Universalist Association's General Assembly; and has been given by many prestigious people, including Martin Luther King, Jr. Vonnegut apparently gave the shortest one in history, to people's dismay and amusement. What people apparently remember most about that lecture, other than its brevity, is that while he spoke he wore a pin with a picture of a sausage in a circle with a line through it: no baloney. The Rev. Tim Jensen also remembers that in the book signing afterwards Vonnegut, after noticing the pen he was using was for Jensen's church in Midland, Texas, kept the pen.[27]

However, if Vonnegut is a Unitarian Universalist, I'm not really sure we want him. After all, in his book *Wampeters, Foma & Grandfalloons*, in the essay, "Yes, We Have No Nirvanas," he said, "Unitarians don't believe in anything. I am a Unitarian."[28] Perhaps he's not our best spokesperson.

Regardless of whether or not we want to claim him, Vonnegut was certainly outspoken on the subject of religion. Unitarian Universalist minister and author Dan Wakefield was a good friend of Kurt Vonnegut, Jr. He writes:

> When I published an article in The New York Times Magazine called "Returning to Church" in 1985, describing my return to the Christianity of my childhood, I got home to find a message on my answering machine.
> "This is Kurt," said the voice of Vonnegut. "I forgive you."[29]

Vonnegut was an avowed atheist and a humanist, as many distinguished Unitarian Universalist have been. He was an honorary president of the American Humanist Association. He often quoted his grandfather, Clemens Vonnegut, whom he regarded as a Free Thinker, as saying, "Whoever entertains liberal views and chooses a consort that is captured by superstition risks his happiness."[30] Vonnegut was critical of religion in some very pointed, and often very humorous ways, but sometimes he is critical of all religions to an extreme. For example, he once said:

How on earth can religious people believe in so much arbitrary, clearly invented balderdash?...The acceptance of a creed, any creed, entitles the acceptor to membership in the sort of artificial extended family we call a congregation. It is a way to fight loneliness. Any time I see a person fleeing from reason and into religion, I think to myself, There goes a person who simply cannot stand being so goddamned lonely anymore."[31]

It is a cynical view of human nature—whereas we might agree with the absolute content, that religion brings people together and forms community, his spin on that is extremely negative.

At other times, however, Vonnegut is very playful about religion. In his short book, *God Bless You, Dr. Kevorkian,* he imagines himself in a lethal injection execution facility, where he is put to death by Dr. Kevorkian so that he might interview people in Heaven, and then he is resuscitated. Vonnegut's Heaven is Universalist—he states clearly that there is no Hell. One of the people he interviews there is Adolph Hitler, who, he writes, "feels remorse for any actions of his, however indirectly, which might have had anything to do with the violent deaths suffered by thirty-five million people during World War II."[32] (Vonnegut had the experience of having fought in World War II—he saw firsthand not only the horrors of the Germans, but also the bombing of Dresden by our forces.) With that experience, it is remarkable that he can be playful with Hitler's character. Playfully, too, Vonnegut interviews a fellow humanist, and another former president of the American Humanist Association, Isaac Asimov, in Heaven. In Heaven, Asimov is working on what he calls a "six-volume set about cockamamie Earthling beliefs in an Afterlife."[33]

I became a Vonnegut fan in college. His irreverence appealed to me in that adolescence. When I look at his writings now, I can see why they were so appealing to me then. However, sometimes his work seems stuck in that adolescence—gratuitous in their use of profanity and sex, seemingly included only for the shock value. He delighted, for example, in the idea that he was the first writer to use the f-word in the title of a story. But we read so much more—and see so much more—these days that's more shocking than Vonnegut's writings, too, that the point is almost missed. It is easy to forget what a fresh voice his was when he first emerged. His writings are certainly products of their times—many of the ones I read were written in the 1970s and 1980s, and indeed, they have a sort of seventies and eighties flair. But there are aspects of his writings that are timeless and profound, as well.

His works are anti-authoritarian, and are an example of pieces of writing that can change the views of a nation. *Slaughterhouse-Five,* which is a fiction work that incorporates many of Vonnegut's experiences during the fire-bombing of Dresden, taught U.S. Americans to look at World War II, and any war, in a new way, much as

Joseph Heller's *Catch-22* did. Vonnegut says in *Slaughterhouse-Five* that it is written by a pillar of salt[34]—comparing himself in profound ways to Lot's wife, who looks back at the destruction of Sodom. He writes of that experience of Dresden, saying,

> Many people see the Dresden massacre as correct and quite minimal revenge for what had been done by the camps. Maybe so. As I say, I never argue that point. I do note in passing that the death penalty was applied to absolutely anybody who happened to be in the undefended city—babies, old people, the zoo animals, and thousands upon thousands of rabid Nazis, of course, and among others, my best friend Bernard V. O'Hare and me. By all rights, O'Hare and I should have been part of the body count. The more bodies, the more correct the revenge."[35]

His scathing critiques of war would be aptly applied to the Iraq War, and indeed many have seen them as applicable. He said, for example, of the war in Iraq:

> By saying that our leaders are power-drunk chimpanzees, am I in danger of wrecking the morale of our soldiers fighting and dying in the Middle East?... Their morale, like so many bodies, is already shot to pieces. They are being treated, as I never was, like toys a rich kid got for Christmas.[36]

Vonnegut, indeed, never stopped talking about current events, never rested on his laurels, and never forgot his roots.

One of the things that I admire about Kurt Vonnegut, Jr., is his support of our first amendment rights. He was a long-time member of the ACLU, and spoke up often about censorship and freedom of the press. When his own book, *Slaughterhouse-Five*, was burned in a furnace in Drake, North Dakota, on orders of the school board, he wrote to the school board directly, saying of his books:

> They beg that people be kinder and more responsible than they often are. It is true that some of the characters speak coarsely. That is because people speak coarsely in real life.... And we all know, too, that those words really don't damage children much. They didn't damage us when we were young. It was evil deeds and lying that hurt us.[37]

I admire Vonnegut for this demand for us to live up to our higher selves—that kinder and more responsible self he mentions.

In reading Kurt Vonnegut, Jr., we bounce from cynical to naïve and from trusting, open, and affirmative to harsh and evil. He puts us in that place between these extremes, and then demands that we respect the inherent worth and dignity of people. It is his refrain; it comes through his works again and again: dignity, dignity, dignity. He writes:

It is easy to see dignity in relatives and friends. It is inevitable that we see it in relatives and friends. What is human dignity, then? It is the favorable opinion, respectful and uncritical, which we hold of those most familiar to us. It has been found that we can hold that same good opinion of strangers, if those who teach us and otherwise lead us tell us to. What could be more essential in pluralistic society like ours than that every citizen see dignity in every other human being everywhere?"[38]

So, yes, I think we should be proud to claim Vonnegut as a Unitarian Universalist. He doesn't speak for all of us—on war, on religion, on God, or on human nature—but he was a free thinker, a radical thinker, and as so belongs to our non-creedal faith of individuals and our profound, sacred, and silly and sacrilegious thoughts, and our inherent worth and dignity.

God bless you, Mr. Vonnegut. So it goes.

Who Do You Say That I Am? Unitarian Universalist Views of Jesus

November 2006
Ohio River Group

Jesus went on with his disciples in the villages of Caesarea Philippi; and on the way he asked his disciples, "Who do people say that I am?" And they answered him, "John the Baptist; and others, Elijah; and still others, one of the prophets." He asked them, "But who do you say that I am?" Peter answered him, "You are the Messiah." And he sternly ordered them not to tell anyone about him. ~ Mark 8:27-30 (NRSV)

Introduction

I was raised as a Unitarian Universalist in a Humanistic Unitarian church by universalist Christian parents (of differing views about the trinity or unity of God). Growing up, I heard little of Jesus in church, but a lot at home. My father, in particular, liked to quote parables to solve squabbles between my sisters and me, as well as to support his own decisions. Particular favorites were the prodigal son and the parable of the workers in the vineyard. As a child, I had a copy of a children's Bible, and many soft-cover children's books that told favorite Bible stories—mostly from Genesis. As I got older, I learned how a universalist Methodist campus minister had influenced my parents' thinking and introduced them to the search for the historical Jesus. My father was particularly motivated by a small book that told what scholars thought was possible and probable for Jesus to have said. The book was T. W. Manson's *The Sayings of Jesus*. Norman Perrin, professor of New Testament at the Divinity School at the University of Chicago, writes in "Rediscovering the Teachings of Jesus by Norman Perrin":

> This is, in effect, a commentary on the material generally ascribed to Q. By today's standards the author accepts material as authentic far too readily...

Manson was absolutely unequalled as an exegete of the teaching of Jesus. His profound knowledge of ancient Judaism, his deep insight into the subject matter, above all, perhaps, his gift of self-expression—all this combines to make the careful reading of this work an unforgettable experience. [39]

"Q" refers to a source gospel, (Quelle, or "source"), which many scholars think was an earlier gospel used by the writers of both the Gospels of Matthew and Luke. Matthew and Luke share some material with Mark, but they also share additional material that is not found in Mark. It is this material that is assumed to come from the lost Q gospel. Perrin's work, which was deeply influential to my father, comes to a very similar conclusion to the later theologians who would hypothesize the existence of Q. What I remember from my father's interpretation of Perrin growing up was that there were things in the gospels that Jesus couldn't have said, because the accounts of his words were contradictory, and not everything could be translated back into the Aramaic language that Jesus spoke.

As I grew up, in about eighth grade, I declared myself to be an atheist. Unfamiliar with agnosticism, I thought this the best match for my beliefs. I later refined my atheistic position to agnostic, and then to incorporate Humanism, as I learned more about the differing terms. My memory of telling my mother about my atheism is a powerful one for me. I was scared of "coming out of the closet" on the subject, and approached it hesitantly. I remember her saying something like, "Oh. I disagree." When I asked her if she thought I was going to Hell, she said, essentially, "No, I still believe you're going to Heaven." (This is an old memory, and her memory of the event is somewhat different.) Her universalism was a deep comfort to me, and the faith of Universalism gives me a deep feeling of universal love and acceptance because of this experience. Looking back, I believe this was a period when I was moving into adolescence and perhaps into what James Fowler calls the "Individuative-Reflective" faith stage.[40] He writes that the movement from a Synthetic-Conventional faith (stage 3) to stage 4 can involve "serious clashes or contradictions between valued authority sources."[41]

When I went to college, I majored in English. The first course, the prerequisite to the major, was "Introduction to Poetry." In this, we read T.S. Eliot's "The Lovesong of J. Alfred Prufrock." The professor explained the references in the poem thoroughly, from the mentions of Michelangelo and Hamlet, to the nod to Marvell's "To His Coy Mistress" with the line "To have squeezed the universe into a ball," and all the other allusions that appear in the poem. However, when we got to the lines about John the Baptist—

But though I have wept and fasted, wept and prayed,
Though I have seen my head [grown slightly bald] brought in upon a platter,
I am no prophet

—he simply said, "That's a reference to John the Baptist, of course." Everyone else in the classroom nodded, and he proceeded onward.

Here I was, with my Unitarian Universalist upbringing—I had no idea who John the Baptist was. He hadn't been in my children's books. I realized it must have something to do with the Bible (the term "Baptist" gave it away), but I didn't even know in what part of the Bible he might appear. I called home that night to find out the answer. This is not to cast dispersions upon my religious education upbringing—I think it was stellar. It is to say that the details of the narrative of Jesus' life had not been given to me with enough regularity that I would have recognized most of it. I knew the birth story, a couple of parables, a few sayings, and that he was crucified, died, and rose from the dead. Granted, part of my ignorance was a real lack of interest. As far as I knew, other than as a teller of parables that could be used to answer children who say, "That's unfair!" he had very little relevance to my life.

Even believing, as I did, that miracles and resurrection were the heart of a very nice piece of fiction, but one I didn't want to read, I embarked upon a study of religion designed to bolster my English studies. One thing led to another, and here I am today, a Unitarian Universalist minister.

But I still had no real interest in Jesus.

Who Do They Say That I Am?

I started with this question: Why are we studying Jesus? My first answer was necessity—for me, I needed to study the Bible as a whole in order to understand our culture, in my case particularly English literature. But this is an unsatisfactory answer. A fairly basic understanding would suffice for this purpose. Why engage in deeper study? Is Jesus relevant to my life at all? Does studying Jesus lead me further on my religious or spiritual path? This led me to more questions: Who is Jesus? Which Jesus are we talking about? What do we, as Unitarian Universalists, believe about Jesus? To look for the answers, I turned to different Unitarian Universalist sources: my family, religious education materials, older books, pamphlets, sermons, and even message boards. To elaborate on the perspectives that Unitarian Universalists hold, I also turned to different Christian theological scholars.

"Who do people say that I am?" Jesus asked his disciples. The disciples give several answers: John the Baptist, Elijah, a prophet. He then asks them who *they* think that he is. Rejecting these answers, Peter says, "the Messiah." The Jesus Seminar gives these lines from Jesus a "black" designation, indicating that they do not believe these to be the actual words of Jesus, stating:

This is a stylized scene shaped by Christian motifs. Jesus rarely initiates dialogue or refers to himself in the first person.

Similar episodes in Thom 13:1-8 and John 1:35-42 indicate how readily the primitive Christian community created scenes like this…Both the story and the words of Jesus are the creation of the story teller in the early Christian movement.[42]

If we did accept, for the purposes of argument, that this is an accurate rendering of an actual conversation, we can say that there were a lot of answers circulating around, even in Jesus' time, as to who he was. What is more likely is that this is a passage that was written not to record a historical conversation, but to further arguments after his death about who Jesus was and what his life meant. There are what could be termed arguments between the gospels, both canonical and Gnostic, about what the primary aspect of Jesus' life and ministry was. Marcus Borg illustrates one piece of this when he writes (about the differing birth narratives): "Matthew emphasizes Jesus' kingship. Luke, with Jesus' genealogy traced back through the prophets, and with the shepherds (who were marginalized) as the ones to whom the news of the birth comes, emphasizes Jesus as a radical social prophet."[43] In *"Who Do Men Say That I Am?"*, a book written as a religious education resource for Unitarians, Susanna Wilder Heinz characterizes Mark as directed towards "those who were not Jewish" and emphasizing human characteristics of Jesus,[44] Matthew as written for Jews and as seeing Jesus as a Messiah and teacher,[45] Luke as focused on explaining Jesus to the Gentiles with an emphasis on the "lowly and downtrodden,"[46] and John as drawing a picture of Jesus that "is not that of a human being, but rather of a being who has existed through eternity and now has come to earth briefly in order to show men how to have faith so that he may be united with God."[47] To add Thomas into this mix is to add a gospel that presents a Jesus who is a teacher and spiritual guide, but gives no evidence of miracles, miraculous birth, or resurrectionIf the gospels writers cannot agree on who Jesus was, then it is much harder for us, millennia later, to decide. Marcus Borg emphasizes four natures of Jesus: spirit person, teacher of wisdom, social prophet, and movement founder.[48] Stephen Prothero focuses on eight portraits of the "American Jesus": the enlightened sage, the sweet savior, the manly redeemer, the superstar, the Mormon elder brother, the Black Moses, the Rabbi, and the Oriental Christ. Susannah Wilder Heinz gives four common views of Jesus: the Crucified Christ, the perfect life, the great religious teacher, and the prophet. The Jesus Seminar states, "The endless proliferation of views of Jesus on the part of those who claim infallibility for the documents erodes confidence in that theological view and in the devotion to the Bible it supports."[49]

Unitarian Universalists have gone beyond just an eroded faith in the infallibility of the Bible, but for Unitarian Universalists, there are still a variety of answers to the question of who Jesus was—and is. For some, Jesus is a purely fictional character. For others, Jesus was a person of historical note, but of very little importance to them now. For many, Jesus was or is a "prophet," although Unitarian Universalists mean many different things by this term. Most Unitarian Universalists would agree that Jesus was a Rabbi, or a teacher. Also, many see him as a great spiritual leader. I want to further examine the different Jesuses that Unitarian Universalists believe in as part of the answer as to why to study him.

Fiction

John Dominic Crossan begins his book *Who Killed Jesus?* with the question of whether the passion accounts are "history remembered" or "prophecy historicized"—that the story of Jesus adapted to fit the prophecies that he would be said to fulfill.[50] Crossan believes that they are prophecy historicized, marking a divergence from many Christian scholars. For many Unitarian Universalists, however, Crossan would still be painting a conservative picture.

Many people believe that Jesus never existed. I remember discussing Jesus with a good friend, an atheist, who loves to bait me about religion, and does so often. He can't understand why I became a minister, and he has difficulty believing, since I'm obviously a minister, that I'm not secretly a Christian, and just not telling him. On one occasion, he pulled out the latest *Time Magazine*, another one with a Jesus cover story for a slow news week, and stated, with firm conviction, that Jesus never existed. I rose to the bait, saying, "But there are historical sources outside of the Bible, which mention him." My friend remained unconvinced. Regardless of Josephus, he was certain that the guy was never there.

This is not an uncommon viewpoint. In *American Jesus*, Stephen Prothero writes about a lecture Rabbi Stephen S. Wise gave in Carnegie Hall in 1925: "Wise began by admitting the reality of the historical Jesus: 'For years I have been led to believe, like thousands of other Jews, that Jesus never existed...I say this is not so. Jesus was.'"[51] Wise's lecture was controversial, not because of his statement that Jesus existed, but because of the way he located Jesus within Judaism. However, his statement about previously believing that Jesus never existed is testimony to the fact that many people, Jews and otherwise, do believe that Jesus is purely fictional.

This view of Jesus exists within Unitarian Universalist circles, as well. An anonymous poster on the forums at the Unitarian Universalist Association website writes, "There is not one shred of evidence for a historical Jesus that hasn't been disproven."[52] While it is arguable from further posts that this writer is not necessarily a Unitarian Universalist, the argument about the existence of Jesus persists.

Another anonymous post states, "It's pure conjecture. There is not one piece of credible evidence that there was a literal Jesus. There is, however, tons of evidence of similar mythological "Jesus" stories in ancient societies thousands of years prior to the start of Christianity."[53]

It is tempting to say that Jesus never existed and leave it at that, particularly as an agnostic Humanist. Certainly, the actual historical Jesus is elusive and fragmentary to us now. But there is too much evidence and too strong a case, I believe, that Jesus did actually exist to dismiss him thusly. My father, William L. Landrum, who believes in Jesus as part of the trinity and considers himself a Unitarian Universalist, has an amusing argument for those who do not believe in Jesus. He writes, "You can argue about the nature of Jesus, how he was born, whether he did any miracles or not, etc.—but not about whether he actually existed or not. It takes a leap of faith of a different sort to jump to that conclusion, that Jesus didn't exist in history."[54]

Jesus without Miracles

Beginning with the supposition that there was a historical Jesus, however, is much more complicated than denying his existence. Once you begin to search for the historical Jesus, you are confronted with all the questions at once, from virgin birth to death and resurrection, and everything in between.

I've spent a lot of time both studying the historical Jesus and talking about him with people, Unitarian Universalist and otherwise, in preparation for this paper. During one car conversation with my mother about the historical Jesus, another relative piped up from the back seat: "Well, we all know what really happened." I'm startled, and curious what it is that "we all know," so I ask, "What?" "He wasn't really dead. They just thought he was," she says.

The different explanations that people have come up with for the miracles and resurrection are legion, from a coma to survivor guilt on the part of the disciples. I have always approached them with an either/or philosophy—if you don't believe they happened as written, then they most likely didn't happen at all. Many others, however, choose a middle approach: parlor magic. Their Jesus is the master magician, fooling the masses with his secret baskets of loaves and fishes or secretly putting the new wine into the old wineskins before the wedding. This Jesus fakes his death in Hollywood style, and does come back after the crucifixion to talk to the disciples. This is not an argument put forth seriously by theologians, but it is similar to the theories put forward by works like *Holy Blood, Holy Grail*, which states, "In short Jesus' apparent and opportune 'demise'—which in the nick of time saves him from certain death and enables him to fulfill a prophecy—is, to say the least, suspect. It is too perfect, too precise to be coincidence. It must either be a later interpolation or part of a carefully conceived plan."[55] There is an attempt by some, Unitarian Universalists among them, to hold to the Bible as a literal historical and accurate account as the writers understood and witnessed, but assuming the writers of the Bible to be fooled. It comes out of a misplaced desire, in my opinion, to cling to Biblical literalism. I find I encounter the same sort of desire in Unitarian Universalists who want to know what the Bible says about homosexuality. While they don't believe in the Bible as the literal word of God generally, they still cling, almost subconsciously, to a belief that the entire Bible has to be believed or disbelieved as a whole. The notion that one could say they believe one part and not another, or that they believe these are the words of Jesus and simply don't agree with them are subtle distinctions that are sometimes missed. Susan Smith writes in "The Truth About Santa," in the *UU World*:

> At some point though, we see that these stories may not be literally true. We "demythologize" old Santa. We can interpret this moment as one of entering into an adult way of knowing, or we may believe that we have been intentionally duped or that the persons who tell this story are ignorant of this "truth." This is Fowler's Stage Four: Individuative-Reflective faith.[56]

I have myself said, and have heard at least one other Unitarian Universalist minister say, that when I learned the truth about Santa, the Easter Bunny, and the Tooth Fairy, I lost faith in God as well. I think Smith's point about the process we go through with Santa is easily compared to our process with Jesus. She quotes Fowler as characterizing Unitarian Universalists as Stage Four adults. This fits with this notion of Jesus entirely.

The Jesus without miracles that I prefer is the one of selectively denying the accuracy of parts of the gospels. This is, too, the work of the Jesus Seminar: to take a scholarly approach and go through the Bible, passage by passage, and determine what Jesus could have said or most likely did not say, voting on each passage's historical accuracy. Voting on the nature of Jesus seems a process tailor-made for Unitarian Universalists, with our belief in the democratic process.

Selective interpretation, particularly in denial of the miracles, is a classic Unitarian approach. Thomas Jefferson gave us his Bible without miracles in our early days, and Unitarian Universalists have been doing it ever since. F. Forrester Church writes in the preface to *The Jefferson Bible*, "When I sat down and actually read *The Life and Morals of Jesus of Nazareth*, I encountered a savior who was born the usual way and died in the usual way. By Jefferson's reading, it was Jesus' unusual life on earth—made unusual by the simple eloquence of his teachings—that truly mattered."[57]

A classic example of the human Jesus, free from miracles, is Sophia Lyon Fahs' 1945 book, *Jesus the Carpenter's Son*, published by Beacon Press. It begins with questions:

> Was Jesus real or was he just a story person? When he was a baby did he know that he was different from all other babies?...Could Jesus do anything he wanted to do? Did he die because he wanted to die, or couldn't he help being killed? Why do we call him Jesus Christ?...Why do some people say he is 'the Son of God'?

Some of these questions are elementary. Others, on the other hand, are ones with which we still struggle.

Fahs does not answer these questions in the book. What she does is present a narrative of Jesus' life. She begins and ends in a way that avoids most of these questions, by omitting Jesus' birth and beginning in his childhood, and by ending with the crucifixion and then jumping to the work of the disciples in beginning the church. By doing these she avoids the questions of birth and resurrection.

Fahs, does, however, in her omission, give a classic view of a Unitarian view of Jesus. In her last chapter, "The End Becomes the Beginning," she states that the followers of Jesus came together to remember the "wonderful experiences they had with Jesus." She pictures them having dreams of Jesus coming back and talking with them, and the dreams are so vivid as to confuse the followers between their dream experiences and their waking ones. She writes:

> Finally, several of them dreamed they saw Jesus rise up from the earth—higher and higher—until he disappeared entirely. They believed he had gone to heaven to be with God. And after that their dreams of seeing him and talking with him stopped.[58]

Thus explaining both resurrection and Pentecost as dreams, she casts Jesus in a fully human role. Lest we think that these views of Jesus are overly simplistic because they are works from the realm of religious education, or that the views are simply dated, I turned to one of our current pamphlets, "UU Views of Jesus." In it, several Unitarian Universalists give quick pictures of who they believe Jesus is and his relevance to our faith. In more poetic language than Fahs, Bruce Southworth gives essentially the same opinion—that the followers of Jesus began to have experiences that they would believe to be true, but that were definitely not immediate experiences of resurrection. He writes: "Following Jesus' death, something happened to the small group of women and men who had chosen to join him. A contagion of love—some transforming, creative event bound them together into a fellowship."[59]

Caroline Landrum, my mother, who has completed several years of seminary and is a self-described "Christian Universalist Unitarian," agrees, and her view may speak for many Unitarian Universalist Christians: "I guess that this is still my belief: that something very transforming happened at the time of the resurrection/Pentecost, so transforming, that it changed the lives of the followers forever and caused them to be bound to the event that did happen and bound to spread the words of this person. It caused them to yell it from the rooftops in such persuasive voices, that many, many more became followers, also. An actual resurrection could be disproved to me, but I would still believe that something dramatic, traumatic, and transforming did happen."[60] This is probably more believable, at least for Unitarian Universalists, than resurrection. But it is also hard to imagine what the "something very transforming" was, exactly. Sophia Lyon Fahs' idea of a series of dreams seems to me to trivialize Jesus, yet anything more miraculous strains my skeptical nature.

In summarizing Unitarian Christian perspectives, Prescott B. Wintersteen writes that Unitarians do not believe in the virgin birth,[61] and says of miracles:

> Jesus' miracles can be accepted or denied. On the one hand, they were the sign of God's acting in and through Christ, and Christ was no ordinary man to be such an agent. The miracles actually occurred, and they were the proof and basis of the Gospels' authority.... On the other hand, they can be dismissed on the ground that all life was a miracle to Jesus, and therefore anything that happened was miraculous. In contradiction: they were not the *proof* of a valid religion, but the exaggerations and misrepresentations of enthusiasts.[62]

While he leaves space for the miracles and sees belief in the miracles as consistent with Unitarianism, many Unitarian Universalists today, Christians as well as non-Christians, do not believe in the miracles. Personally, I have not ever really believed in the miracles of Jesus.

Why do so many Unitarian Universalists deny the miracles, when so many others believe in them? As a Humanist, denying the miracles fits my theology, but is this simply bending the world to fit my belief system? The fact is, from Jefferson onward, Unitarian Universalists have taken this view of Jesus' life not only because there is no external source that speaks of the miracles, but because they're simply hard to believe. It is easy to believe that the miracles were added later. In an article by Erik Reece titled "Jesus Without the Miracles," Reece draws together Jefferson's Bible, the Gospel of Thomas, and Ralph Waldo Emerson to argue for a cohesive Jesus without miracles that he can find worthy of following:

> And whereas Jefferson found in Jesus' teaching an ethic for how we should treat others, Emerson found in it an alchemical light that transforms flesh

into spirit. In some uncanny trick of history and geography, the ancient Gospel of Thomas combines these two visions of Jesus to give us what I would call a truly American gospel.[63]

Once the miracles, birth narrative, and resurrection are removed from the tale of Jesus, is the remaining narrative compelling enough to warrant millennia of study and worship? What we are left with is a view of an extraordinary person, but a person nonetheless. Even without the miracles, one can believe that Jesus was closer to God and had deeper insights than, perhaps, Aristotle or any other great thinker. But for the Humanists, atheists, and agnostics in Unitarian Universalism, while Jesus may have had particular insight, the "closer to God" argument for his study cannot hold the focus. I turn, then, to three aspects of Jesus that do warrant further study.

The Historical Jesus: Prophet, Teacher, Spiritual Leader

Jesus said to his disciples, "Compare me to someone and tell me whom I am like." ~ Thomas 18:1[64]
Jesus the Prophet: *Simon Peter said to him, "You are like a righteous messenger." ~ Thomas 18:2*[65]

Turning to the pamphlets, the true Unitarian Universalist canon, I find Alice Blair Wesley's answer to who Jesus was: "Among us, Jesus' very human life and teaching have been understood as products of, and in line with, the great Jewish tradition of prophets and teachers. He neither broke with that tradition nor superseded it."[66] (I beg to differ; Jesus broke with the tradition all over the place.) To quote a few more examples of the prophetic view of Jesus, Guy C. Quinlan of All Souls, New York, offers: "Jesus carried forward the Jewish prophetic tradition that finds the essence of religion in doing justice. For him, as for Amos and Isaiah, religious observance without social justice was a blasphemous mockery."[67] Kristin Jewett Harper writes, "The man called Jesus of Nazareth was the inheritor of the Hebrew prophetic tradition of bearing witness to justice, the primacy of ethical living in community, and the possibility of reformation for all. His life was an example of the supremacy of human agency, as well as the model of struggle for healing and recognition of the inherent worth and dignity of the poor and oppressed."[68]

This seems to be one of the most common views of the historical Jesus among Unitarian Universalists—and it is not a new one. Susannah Wilder Heinz writes of those who see this view of Jesus:

Some of them say that Jesus was the greatest prophet of them all, while others point to the long line of prophets in the Old Testament. Amos, Hosea, Isaiah, Jeremiah are in the great prophetic tradition. To some, Jesus stands in this tradition. When they look at the pages of the New Testament, they see again the same kind of impatience, with hypocrisy and superficiality and disdain of God's will, which is focused in the pages of the Old Testament. Those who picture Jesus as a prophet hear one single prophetic voice which speaks to our time.[69]

When Unitarian Universalists speak of Jesus as prophet, usually we are redefining the word prophet, as well. Unlike the commonly understood definition of "A person who speaks by divine inspiration or as the interpreter through whom the will of a god is expressed,"[70] Unitarian Universalists, while sometimes accepting this definition, often mean a much milder definition of prophet as akin to "social activist." The root of the word "prophet" shows the meaning as "one who speaks before," but does not necessarily imply knowledge from God.

The popularity of this view of Jesus is easily understood. Unitarian Universalists who see themselves as social activists are quick to see Jesus in the same role. Whether one considers oneself Christian or not, and whether or not one finds Jesus to be a source of inspiration for one's own religious journeys, Jesus is the ultimate religious and moral authority for many *other* people. It is therefore useful for Unitarian Universalist social activists to be able to claim that Jesus was "one of our own." As a faith with a large number of activists in it, the predominance of this view of Jesus is logical. Certainly there is great precedence for this view of Jesus in liberation theologies.

This view is easily supported and documented. First, in the liberation theologies, the view of Jesus as advocate for the oppressed is held up as central. Likewise, for those who search for the historical Jesus, evidence for Jesus as the social prophet is available as well. Bruce Chilton writes of Jesus as a "mamzer": "In the absence of proof, Jesus was considered a *mamzer*, what the Mishnah at a slightly later period calls a *shetuqi*, or "silenced one"...without a voice in the public congregations that regulated the social, political, and religious life of Israel."[71] Locating Jesus as an outcast is one way to create an image of Jesus who will become a prophetic voice for social change. Stephen Prothero, in *American Jesus*, gives one powerful example of locating Jesus in a place of oppression in order to create a vision of Jesus as a leader of modern social movements. Prothero quotes the Rev. Henry McNeal Turner, an African Methodist Episcopal Church bishop as saying in 1898:

Every race of people since time began who have attempted to describe God by words, or by paintings, or by carvings, or by any other form or figure, have conveyed the idea that the God who made themselves and shaped their destinies was symbolized in themselves, and why should not the Negro believe that he resembles God as much so as other people? We do not believe that there is any hope for a race of people who do not believe that they look like God.[72]

Indeed. Unitarian Universalists are doing much the same thing in casting their view of the prophet Jesus—creating a God who looks like them. That Jesus died for his radical social views is another aspect of this version of Jesus that makes it compelling. The problem is that it makes Jesus just another figure in the line of other social justice martyrs, such as the Rev. Dr. Martin Luther King, Jr.

This is a tempting view of Jesus, but perhaps too easy. The picture that is emerging of the historical Jesus is one of a social change agent in his time, but the forces he was seeking to change were very different from today's realities. The Jewish purity system is described by many modern scholars as the focus for Jesus' prophetic witness. Bruce Chilton writes, "He also had a deep conviction that the people he invited to cleanse themselves by immersion were *already* clean. That was why he could eat with them; within the Judaism of his time, eating with people was vivid testimony that one considered them to be pure."[73] Marcus Borg writes of Jesus as indicting primarily the purity system, as well: "Jesus spoke of purity as on the inside and not on the outside: 'There is nothing outside a person that by going in can defile, but the things that come out are what defile.' To say that purity is a matter of what is inside is radically to subvert a purity system constituted by external boundaries."[74]

Borg applies Jesus' attack on the purity system to l/g/b/t rights by saying:

> I am convinced that much of the strongly negative attitude toward homosexuality on the part of some Christians has arisen because, in addition to whatever nonreligious homophobic reasons may be involved, homosexuality is seen (often unconsciously) as a purity issue. For these Christians, there's something "dirty" about it, boundaries are being crossed, things are being put together that do not belong together, and so forth. Indeed, homosexuality was a purity issue in ancient Judaism. The prohibition against it is found in the purity laws of the book of Leviticus.[75]

Borg's argument is a compelling one. However, I believe it is too easy to take Jesus out of the context of the history of his time and apply his teachings to today's culture. Ultimately, it is impossible to know the answer to the question "What Would Jesus Do?" The conservatives think he would lead their agenda just as the liberals do. As the members of the Jesus Seminar caution, "Beware of finding a Jesus entirely congenial to you."[76]

Finally, for me, the argument that Jesus would do this or that if he were alive today is not one which is terribly significant. When one views Jesus as fully human, he can be as wrong as the next person.

Jesus the Teacher: *Matthew said to him, "You are like a wise philosopher." ~ Thomas 13:377*

Another, perhaps equally common, view of Jesus within Unitarian Universalist circles is that of Jesus as teacher, or Rabbi. The Unitarian Universalist Church of Nashua says on their website, "Most UUs [Unitarian Universalists] view Jesus as a moral and ethical teacher and no more than that."[78] Our colleague the Rev. Jennifer Owen-O'Quill, writes, "Throughout the Gospels Jesus the man is a holy teacher, a healer, a prophet and a preacher. He travels far and wide with his disciples sharing his message."[79]

That Jesus is a teacher is evident through his rhetoric. Stephen Funk, in *Honest to Jesus*, ably demonstrates how Jesus uses antithetical couplets, typification, caricature, and reversal, paradoxes, case parodies, parody of symbols, humor, and everyday logic in his rhetoric.[80]

Jesus is often referred to as a Rabbi, and one of the aspects of a Rabbi is a teacher. I don't disagree with the portrayal of Jesus as a teacher, but the question is, teacher of what? Aside from spiritual teachings, Jesus is a teacher of the tradition, breaking with the current teaching of his times in dramatic and significant ways, but like many teachers trying to realign his students with the right path. Jesus is also a teacher of morals and ethics, as mentioned above.

This Jesus I find meaningful, and this teaching is relevant to my life, my ministry, and my congregation. For example, in the parable of the workers in the vineyard (Matthew 20:1-16), where the workers who arrive later in the day are paid equally to the ones who arrive earlier, prompting the earlier workers to complain, I find meaningful applications to today's situations, from the recent ballot proposal against affirmative action in Michigan to the need for a living wage and the worker's rights campaign of the Unitarian Universalist Service Committee.

At the same time, however, I don't believe *all* of Jesus' teachings. When one does not accord him special authority as a messiah or a direct conduit to God, his teachings, while eloquent and meaningful, can be used or discarded as one sees fit. Ultimately, this is the struggle with Jesus: to be free to *not* accept parts of his teaching in a culture where to speak of him at all is to assume his infallibility. Furthermore, not only do I not believe all his teachings, many of his teachings can be given disparate readings, and it is unclear from the start which really are his teachings.

Where does that leave us, then, in a desire to use Jesus as an ethical and moral teacher, or a teacher of the tradition? Yes, the stories and parables make handy sermon illustrations. They have become part of the cultural narrative and source from which we draw. However, I feel free to say I disagree at times, as well.

Jesus the Spiritual Leader: *Peter responds to him, "You are the Anointed!"* ~ *Mark 8:29*81

One final view of Jesus is as the great spiritual leader, or at least *a* great spiritual leader. Susannah Wilder Heinz paints a picture of this belief:

> Others have told us of the Great Religious Teacher. In their search through the sacred writings of many religions, they have found the same ethical and spiritual truths repeated again and again. On occasion, however, a religious leader shares with his followers new insights which reveal another facet of truth. Such a man was Gautama Buddha, such a man Confucius, such a man Mohammed. So also was Jesus. Each gathered about him disciples who carried forward his teaching until, as succeeding generations followed one after another, the man himself became obscured in myth and legend. To uncover once more the truths which these men revealed, and to come close to them as human beings, is to add another stone to the ever enlarging, never to be finished, building of religious knowledge.[82]

A similar portrait of Jesus can be seen in this quote from Alice Blair Wesley: "Many of us honor Jesus, and many of us honor other master teachers of past or present generations, like Moses or the Buddha. As a result, mixed-tradition families may find common ground in the UU [Unitarian Universalist] fellowship without compromising other loyalties."[83] Stephen Kendrick sees Jesus as not just a spiritual leader, but goes on to say, "Jesus has taught me not to worship false idols, but rather the Divine Love that broods over all and lives inside each. This sort of love requires a tradition of openness, tolerance, freedom, and radical compassion."[84]

This Jesus is the Jesus that we place beside Mohammed, the Buddha, and other religious and spiritual leaders. He is the Jesus that sparks the movement. No one can argue that this Jesus does not exist, in that the movement exists, but it is arguable whether Jesus intended to create such a Christianity as exists today or in the past. At the same time, it is clear that Jesus had a religious message for his followers.

I find it impossible, however, as a Humanist and Agnostic, to simply say that I see Jesus as a great spiritual leader. Jesus' spirituality does not speak to me in this way. I do not find that his words guide me on a path closer to the ground of all being. While he has been this kind of force in so many people's lives, I do not connect to him at this level.

Who Do I Say That He Is?

Thomas said to him, "Master, my mouth is utterly unable to say what you are like."
Jesus said, "I am not your master. Because you have drunk, you have become intoxi-
cated from the bubbling spring that I have tended." ~ Thomas 13:4-5[85]

Who is the Jesus, then, with whom I am left? Clearly, Jesus is a figure that is of great importance in our culture. Just as clearly, there are many different and divergent viewpoints as to who he was. Even the Jesus Seminar resorts to voting on what passages they find to be his authentic voice.

As an illustration, I have a good friend who was a very active Harry Potter fan, and who participated in on-line forums to discuss the characters in this series of children's books. Of particular interest to her was one character, Snape, and whether he is good or evil, and what his motivation is. In this case, there is a living author, but one who was being cagey about her creations due to a desire to leave the mysteries of the final book to unfold after publication. The on-line community relentlessly debated the nature of this character, and divided into different factions, with different spaces carved out for them in cyberspace. There was no general agreement on who Severus Snape is, and what his actions meant. Some saw him as a hero, others as a villain.

In the gospels, we have books of unclear authorship written probably decades to even centuries after the events of one, arguably historical, person's life. Josephus wrote his accounts from the mid-70s to 90s CE; Mark, the earliest gospel, was written after 74 CE; and John may be as late as 90 CE.[86] Marcus Borg writes of the gospels:

> Written in the last third of the first century, they contain the accumulated traditions of early Christian communities and were put into their present form by second- (or even third-) generation authors. Through careful comparative study of the gospels, one can see these authors at work, modifying and adding to the traditions they received. They were continuing a process that had been going on through-out the forty to seventy years when the gospel material circulated in oral form. Much happened in these decades to change the traditions about Jesus.[87]

Furthermore, even after the gospels were written, they went through multiple hands before they reached us. The Jesus Seminar authors write:

> The oldest surviving copies of the gospels date from about one hundred and seventy-five years after the death of Jesus, and no two copies are precisely alike. And handmade manuscripts have almost always been "corrected" here

and there, often by more than one hand. Further, this gap of almost two centuries means that the original Greek (or Aramaic?) text was copied more than once, by hand, before reaching the stage in which it has come down to us.[88]

I believe that no matter how compelling the gospels may be, there is no way to know its accuracy in depicting the real man who lived and breathed. The Jesus Seminar's votes show a belief that only 18% of the sayings attributed to Jesus were actually spoken by him.[89] Furthermore, so much of his message directly related to the historical and religious context in which he lived, that I question the rightness of applying it to our context today. I cannot with any certainty say that Jesus would believe in gay rights, abortion, or evolution. I cannot say he wouldn't, either. The best I can do is say that of all the different pictures of Jesus that have been painted, the ones that I find compelling, the ones that I find the most interesting, are these modern Unitarian Universalist pictures of a social prophet and ethical teacher.

Understanding the nature of Jesus, the character of Jesus, has been central for me in trying to understand why we study him. But I realize that while my faith as a whole may have moved on, the Jesuses I've discussed have been from a "Individuative-Reflective" faith stance. The challenge for me, as for many Unitarian Universalists, is how to integrate Jesus into a faith like Fowler's Stage 5, Conjunctive Faith, in which there is "a new reclaiming and reworking of one's past" in which "symbols, myths and rituals...have been grasped, in some measure, by the depth of reality to which they refer,"[90] or Stage 6, Universalizing Faith, in which we become more like Jesus himself, the rare "incarnators and actualizers of the spirit of an inclusive and fulfilled human community."[91] To really study Jesus should be to move beyond even the painstaking and important work of the Jesus Seminar, probing and searching for the historical Jesus, and to realize that all these different Jesuses are myths—symbols—which point to the deeper way. Why do we study Jesus? The narratives we tell, including those of Jesus, are the real living tradition that we share, whether from "once upon a time" to "happily ever after" or from "in the beginning" to "amen."

———

"Who do you say that I am?" We hear the disciples' answers. But on this question, Jesus remains silent. It is up for us to interpret, to answer for ourselves, and to live that reality.

Part 2
Faith through Justice

The Religious Importance of Tolerance

January 11-12, 2003
The Gardner News

In 1557, in Romania, Queen Isabella decreed that each person could "maintain whatever religious faith he wishes, with old and new rituals" and that it was up to each person's judgment "to do as they please in the matter of faith, just so long, however, as they bring no harm to bear on anyone."[92] It was the first decree of its kind, and allowed religious freedom, as well as freedom of belief. In England, in 1689, the Parliament passed the Act of Toleration. The Act of Toleration made it lawful again for "nonconformists, other than Catholics and deniers of the Trinity, to hold public worship," according to Charles A. Howe, author of *For Faith and Freedom.*[93] Here in the United States of America, we, too, have a country which is based in freedom of religion and freedom of belief. The First Amendment of the Constitution, adopted in 1791, states: "Congress shall make no law respecting an establishment of religion, or prohibiting the free exercise thereof." Freedom of belief is something we often take for granted in the United States of America. However, as sacred as it is to us, we are letting it erode all the time.

This year has been one where we've seen many acts of religious intolerance. Muslims and Sikhs throughout this country have been harassed for their religious beliefs. This is not a new thing, however. Other groups in this country, too, have been persecuted in the name of religion, such as gay, lesbian, bisexual, and transgendered people. Most often, this has been done in the name of God, or in the name of country. Yet these actions go against both God, from almost any theistic religion's perspective, and country.

I believe that freedom of religion is not just a civic or political issue. It is a fundamentally religious issue. We are called by our own faith, whatever it is, to support it. It is not just "political correctness" to require the acceptance and tolerance of diversity. Almost every major religion in this world has some equivalent to the Golden Rule: Do unto others as you would have them do unto you. Another way of phrasing this might be, "Treat others as you think they would want you to."

I myself am not a practicing Christian, but I believe that regardless of one's religious beliefs, everyone can learn something from Jesus' parable of the Good Samaritan. Jesus preached that people should love their neighbors. When asked, "Who is my neighbor?" Jesus responded with a story of a man who was beaten and robbed and left for dead. The priest who passed him did not help, and neither did the Levite. Both of these were devout people, and native people, who might have been expected to help. Instead, the wounded man was helped by a Samaritan. A Samaritan was a foreigner, and would not have been expected to help a Jew in those times. The Samaritan, Jesus explained, was this man's neighbor. This is who you should love.

Who, then, is our neighbor? The words of Jesus call people to love their non-native neighbors, and their neighbors of differing faiths. Who are the Samaritans to me? Who are the Samaritans to you? In this country, as religious and ethnic minorities, clearly Arab and Muslim people are neighbors to the majority of us.

Whatever your religious path, there's a need for each of us to sometimes let go of anger, hatred, and fear. Xenophobia, fear of foreigners and strangers, is something we're all faced with at times. We can easily become suspicious of things we don't understand. We must remember that the foreigner or stranger is our neighbor, and that we must love him or her. In this time of war, we have too many intense feelings of anger and hatred running hot. Instead, we need to focus on tolerance, diversity, and love. It is our standing on these principles of openness and acceptance that makes this country strong. Our country is founded upon religious diversity and freedom of religion—we, as a nation, deplore the rigidity of requiring acceptance to a strict doctrine of beliefs expressed by others. Let us not accept, in retaliation to terrorism, the same closed-minded attitude towards others' differences.

Everyday Heroism

May 2, 2010
Universalist Unitarian Church of East Liberty
Clarklake, MI

Every year brings provocative questions from congregation members. This time, a member has asked me to talk about everyday heroism and everyday spirituality.

There's a connection to be made just in the question of how we define heroism, and how we define spirituality. Heroism is often used in our culture in a way that equates it with extraordinary accomplishments—great actors, sports figures or musicians might be said to be someone's personal hero. The television show "Heroes" uses this definition somewhat, as its main characters are all people with super capabilities, like the superheroes in comic books. However, both those fictional characters and our actors, politicians and sports heroes don't always evidence heroic qualities—actions and values—to go along with the superpowers or culturally-valued athletic or popularity achievements.

Heroism, at a better definition, is defined by the willingness to put oneself in harm's way in order to benefit another. Heroism can be saving someone from drowning, or standing up to a bully; these carry physical risks for doing the right thing. Heroism can also be whistle-blowing, when it risks your job, or saying no when being asked to perform work that harms or degrades another, at risk, again, of loss of livelihood. By this measure, someone like Captain Sullenberger, the pilot who managed to navigate an emergency plane landing on the Hudson River, would not necessarily fall under the definition of heroism. He did not actually chose to put himself in harm's way in order to benefit others; he would've incurred greater personal risk by not landing the plane thusly, and so by doing this admittedly remarkable action, he saved his own life as well as the lives of others. But that's not the kind of heroism I'm talking about here with this definition of heroism. The distinction is subtle, but important.

The link between our definitions of everyday heroism and everyday spirituality, is just like we may think of heroism as being the remarkable, we may also think of spirituality as having to be the remarkable. We may think of spirituality as that moment of shining grace where God's voice breaks through the clouds, or of spiritual places as only the grandest cathedrals, or of spiritual acts as only those of the Mother Theresas. Similarly, spirituality, as I'm defining it, is by its nature an everyday, go now and live your religion today and tomorrow and next week kind of thing. In believing as we do in this faith in our interconnection, and the sacredness of all life, and in the spark of the divine in each of us, this democratic faith places this spirituality in all of us and in every day, just as the potential for heroism lies within all of us.

The member who posed the topic of everyday heroism linked the topic to a quote by Miep Gies. Miep Gies helped hide Anne Frank and her family in the annex during the Holocaust, and saved Anne's diary to give to Mr. Frank after the war ended. Miep Gies resisted the term hero, because she didn't want people to think you had to be someone special to do what she did. She wanted it to be understood that this was something anyone could do. She said, "I don't want to be considered a hero. Imagine young people would grow up with the feeling that you have to be a hero to do your human duty. I am afraid nobody would ever help other people, because who is a hero? I was not. I was just an ordinary housewife and secretary."

It makes complete sense to me that if you want to study everyday heroism, you need to start with the Holocaust. For me, the Holocaust was the beginning of my moral and ethical questioning, and my questioning about the nature of humanity. It all started with a class I took in high school on Holocaust literature. At the foundation of Holocaust literature are deep questions about humanity: Are we essentially good or evil? What makes us into people who are willing to commit genocide? What makes us into people who will enter into these acts of heroism? Fundamentally, where do I stand?

In looking at the question of what Hannah Arendt called "the banality of evil," in my high school class we studied some classic examples of how ordinary, everyday citizens became people who would oppress their fellow citizens. We studied the "Brown Eyes, Blue Eyes" experiment with schoolchildren who when told that one eye color was superior, almost instantly started oppressing their fellow classmates. We studied the "Stanford Prison Experiment," where college students were classified into prisoners or guards and eventually the abuse perpetrated by the guard-students on the prisoner-students became so horrible that the experiment had to be shut down. Likewise, Daniel Jonah Goldhagen's book, *Hitler's Willing Executioners: Ordinary Germans and the Holocaust*, makes the point that the Holocaust couldn't have happened without the willing participation of the vast number of Germans involved. He writes, "It is also likely that disapproving individuals, finding themselves in an *atmosphere of general approval*, would, because of group pressure, commit acts which they had considered to be crimes."[94] His point is that while some individual Germans would have gone along with the Holocaust because of fear of disobeying, or because of group pressure, it was necessary for the majority of the group, the majority of the Germans carrying out the Holocaust, to be in agreement with it.

Looking at situations like these, it is easy to believe that our human nature is to devolve into this banality of evil whenever we're put under the stress of the system. The questions learning those studies awoke in me—Are we essentially evil? Would I, in the same circumstance, do the same?—have stayed with me a lifetime. They prompted me to make sure that I did everything I could to be someone who would stand up against injustice, and who would dedicate my life to the pursuit of the good. But still unanswered was the question of what made someone step up into the role of heroism at personal risk. Is that person a real exception, far outside of the norm? Or is that person an everyday person, as heroism is something that even the most ordinary person can do?

The answers are yes, and yes, I think. It is not the norm for people to make personal risks to save another, even though heroes will often tell you they just did what anyone would do. It is an exception, when you understand that your own livelihood or life is on the line. We know bystanders will often just stand by. But, at the same time, the potential to be a hero is something that each and every person carries. We all carry the spark of heroism within us. We all could be Miep Gies if put in such a situation. For these reasons, Miep Gies was both wrong and right. She was right to think that what she did was something that anyone could do. But she was wrong to think that she was not heroic—she was. Not everyone chooses the path of heroism. The Holocaust teaches us this.

If my Holocaust literature course has haunted me for a lifetime, I think Philip Zimbardo, the professor who ran the Stanford Prison Experiment, is even more haunted. What I found very moving is that he has moved from the question that the Stanford Prison Experiment exposed of how we can all become the face of evil to the question of what prompts us, what traits or experiences call us, to become the everyday hero. Regarding this, Zimbardo wrote in his article, "For Goodness' Sake":

> What is it, then, that enables some people to refuse to participate in or condone wrongdoing? In part, it is their sensitivity to situational pressures (being aware when someone is trying to con them), and their willingness to be rejected by the group when they know they're right. They know intuitively how to spot and identify wolves dressed in sheep's garments (the sweet-talking cult recruiter or the friendly neighbor who wants you to help discourage a gay couple from moving in next door). They're also aware of how their own thinking can distort what's going on around them (as when you want something so badly—say, a promotion, or other people's acceptance—that you ignore the warning signs that something's not right with what you're being asked to do to get it).[95]

In another article, "The Banality of Heroism," Zimbardo gives a list of ways to prepare oneself to be an everyday hero. His steps are: 1) Always remain mindful; critically evaluate situations. 2) Don't fear interpersonal conflict. 3) Look beyond present situations to the long term. 4) "Resist the urge to rationalize inaction and to develop justifications that recast evil deeds as acceptable means to supposedly righteous ends." Lastly, 5) Transcend the thoughts of the negative consequences that come with action.[96]

What Zimbardo teaches me in this is that heroism—this everyday heroism that we are capable of, each and every one of us—is something that has to be encouraged, cultivated and nurtured within our individual souls.

Finally, here's the connection to spirituality, and specifically to our faith: To grow your potential for heroism, you have to grow your soul. You have to grow your critical mind, your compassion, and your willingness to be outside the norm. As Emerson said, "Whoso would be a man must be a nonconformist." That's it, exactly: To be the kind of people who have true character, truly heroic natures, we must be, in Emerson's word, nonconformists.

We often want to set aside heroes as out-of-the-ordinary, because it relieves us, in a way, of the pressure to make our lives extraordinary, to make our lives heroic. We want the easy road, not the hard one.

The spiritual masters have been trying to teach us this harder path for centuries. That's right: spiritual practice takes practice. Spirituality isn't always easy. Buddhist master Thich Nhat Hahn's *The Miracle of Mindfulness* teaches us to pay attention every day to the little things that we do, and to do them mindfully, such as peeling an orange or doing the dishes, and to not be thinking about or doing something else when we're peeling an orange, but to really peel the orange. This is Zimbardo's first step of remaining mindful and critical. The practice of solitude and meditation, found in many religions, gives people the fortitude to withstand groupthink and peer-pressure, and the willingness to step outside the norms and risk being alone. Here are the words of a follower of Thich Nhat Hahn about solitude:

> Although in our daily lives we are constantly with the Sangha, we are also in solitude. Solitude is not about being alone high up in the mountains, or in a hut deep in the forest, it is not about hiding ourselves away from civilization. Real solitude comes from a stable heart that does not get carried away by the crowd nor by our sorrows about the past, our worries about the future, and our excitement about the present. We do not lose ourselves; we do not lose our mindfulness.[97]

This passage takes the idea of solitude and meditation and connects it to several of Zimbardo's principles for fostering heroism. First, solitude is about not always going with the crowed, and being comfortable being alone. Second, solitude is about not getting caught up in the moment.

In our closing song every week we sing, "Go now and live your religion; its truth reflect in all you do." We are giving ourselves a religious order every week, and that religious order is to risk being a hero when heroism is called for. This is at the heart of our religion, and it's our everyday practice—our spiritual practice—to walk in this world in a way consistent with our ethical and religious teachings.

It is not easy to do. I think it can also be particularly difficult for our children, because peer pressure is very strong when you're a child. It is very important at young ages to fit in and gain the acceptance of a group, and our religion often steps people outside of the group. We don't teach children in our religious education classes to believe in Jesus and the resurrection; we let them learn about those things and then decide for themselves. The same is true of how we teach about God. As someone who grew up in a Unitarian Universalist church with a religious education program like this, let me tell you it was often very hard. It is hard when your school friends are pressuring you to believe what they believe, to go to their church or their church camp or their church programs. It is hard to be honest and truthful about what you believe in the face of that and to not conform.

But it is important that we are training our children to think for themselves, and to not just take whatever answer is thrust upon them. It is important that our children are learning to stand sometimes a bit outside of the norm. It is important that our children learn to not fear the small conflicts that come with standing up for who they are.

Because, friends, we are training them in our faith and churches to be heroes—everyday heroes. This is what our faith is about for young and old alike. We ask you to be heroes.

Go now and live your religion.

The Gaping Chasm

March 15-16, 2003
The Gardner News

The Rev. Dr. Martin Luther King, Jr. once said, "Before it is too late, we must narrow the gaping chasm between our proclamations of peace and our lowly deeds which precipitate and perpetuate war. One day we must come to see that peace is not merely a distant goal that we seek but a means by which we arrive at that goal."

There are many different political views about what needs to be done about war in Iraq, just as there have been many different views of all wars and potential wars. Neither those who believe in the cause of war nor those who hold out for peaceful means can have their views summarized in a simple sentence or paragraph. However, despite the complexity of the issue, I believe that everyone, in his or her heart, wants peace. The difference is in how people think peace can be achieved.

Politics is not my field. However, religion is. Indeed, when we use words like "evil" and talk about God blessing this nation, we are invoking religious arguments for political causes. If there is one thing I am sure of, it is that religion is about peace, and should not be used for war.

There have been, of course, many wars fought in the name of religion. The crusades are among the most famous. Obviously thousands of people have been killed in the name of religion; including those executed in our country for witchcraft. But to use religion as an instrument of death is to subvert the message and the meaning of that which is most sacred and holy.

All the religious heroes in my life and in so many others'—the Rev. Dr. Martin Luther King, Jr., Unitarian author Henry David Thoreau, Hindu leader Mahatma Gandhi, Catholic Mother Theresa, and so many more from different religious traditions—have taught us lessons of peace, of patience, of love, of caring. These wise souls cry out to us about the importance of peace, and about possibility.

The book of Proverbs from the Jewish and Christian scriptures states, "Happy are those who find wisdom...Her ways are ways of pleasantness, and all her paths are peace." (3:1, 17). All the wisdom paths are peaceful, and the paths of other religions echo this. The path of religion is the path of peace.

For those who believe in God, one way to look at it is this: God values life. God values one single human life more than the security of our country, more than our access to oil, more than our pride, more than our economic gain.

This war we face, like so many others, pits one religion against another, in many people's minds—a Christian nation against a Muslim nation. But both religions are religions of peace, not of war. It is those who are listening first to other needs—political, social, economic—which cry for war. The five pillars of Islam, after all, include charity and prayer, not war. The Koran states: "Fight for the sake of God those that fight you, but do not attack them first. God does not love the aggressors." In other words, God commands people to fight only in self-defense. A traditional saying of the prophet Mohammed is, "Shall I not inform you of a better act than fasting, alms, and prayers? Making peace between one another: enmity and malice tear up heavenly rewards by the roots." The saying of Mohammed echoes that of Jesus: "The greatest of these is love," while telling us that peace is the path to Heaven. The Bible, too, mentions peace often, and Jesus is known, among other names, as "the Prince of Peace."

In the words of the Rev. Dr. Martin Luther King, Jr., "We must pursue peaceful ends through peaceful means." Every religion gives us the call. Every spiritual path tells us this is the road. It may not be the political answer, but it is the religious one. The soul path, the heart path, the path of the spirit is the path of peace.

You've Got to Be Carefully Taught

January 17, 2010
Universalist Unitarian Church of East Liberty
Clarklake, MI

> You've got to be taught
> Before it's too late
> Before you are 6 or 7 or 8
> To hate all the people
> your relatives hate
> You've got to be carefully taught.
> —Rodgers and Hammerstein,
> "You've Got to Be Carefully Taught," *South Pacific*

We know, and have known, that racism can be taught. As a high school student, I studied the 1968 case of teacher Jane Elliot who divided her third-grade class into brown-eyed people and blue-eyed people, and informed them that blue-eyed people were better and gave them special privileges—the blue-eyed children got more recess and they got to use the water fountain, whereas the brown-eyed children had to use paper cups. Jane Elliot said of the experiment, "I watched what had been marvelous, cooperative, wonderful, thoughtful children turn into nasty, vicious, discriminating little third-graders in a space of fifteen minutes."[98] She also noticed that the students' scores went down when they were the group on the bottom, and went up when they were the group on the top.

We have a belief in our society that children are born as a blank slate, John Locke's *tabula rasa*, that we are free from prejudice, and that prejudice is something we have to be, as the song tells us, carefully taught. We want to believe that if we raise our children in a neutral, multiracial environment, that they will become prejudice-free adults. A lot of parents agonize about what school to put their children in—torn between wanting diverse, multicultural environments, and high academic standards and high test scores, and these things don't always go hand-in-hand. I know Peter and I, when choosing a school for our daughter, looked at all these things. Some schools we rejected outright—we just couldn't bring ourselves to put her in the public school that was 95% white, opting for the more multiracial school that was 61% white. It ranked three percent lower test scores in English than that 95% white school, but one percent higher in math.

Not only do we, in our society have the attitude that the most important thing to do to combat racism is to put our children in diverse environments, sometimes we do this to the exclusion of anything else. We have a deep reluctance to talking about race in our society, particularly amongst those who wish to raise their children without racism. In *NurtureShock*, the authors talk about a study done by Birgitte Vittrup at the University of Texas, which divided parents and children into three groups. One group was just asked to watch multicultural videos. The second group they watched the multicultural videos, and the parents were also asked to talk to their children about race. The third group had no videos, but were also given a checklist of topics and asked to talk about race without any videos prompting the discussion. Bronson and Merryman report, "At this point, something interesting happened. Five of the families in the last group abruptly quit the study. Two directly told Vittrup, 'We don't want to have these conversations with our child. We don't want to point out skin color.'"[99]

At the end of the study, Vittrup's numbers seemed to show that there was no positive effect of the parents talking to children about race from the ones who hadn't. But then when she looked at her results more closely, she discovered something—most of the families had avoided doing the instructions as much as possible—they had only mentioned the items on her list briefly and in passing. The children of the few who did talk about it showed improved attitudes.[100]

It is hard to talk to your children about race. My parents have an embarrassing story about when they started to talk to me about race, jumping in and saying something just as I was about to say something embarrassing. I had this same experience with my daughter. In NurtureShock the authors write, "Over the course of our research, we heard many stories of how people—from parents to teachers—were struggling to talk about race with their children. For some, the conversations came up after a child had made an embarrassing comment in public. A number had the issue thrust on them, because of interracial marriage or an international adoption. Still others were just introducing children into a diverse environment, wondering when and if the timing was right."[101]

I know first hand how awkward and uncomfortable it can be to talk to your child about race. I admit it felt awkward and uncomfortable when my child started coming home full of discussion about racism. She had gotten this information from our own religious education classes, so I knew it was being taught in a way sensitive to our values. But I was still unsure what to say when she said, seemingly out of the blue to me, "Mama, a long time ago it was dark-skinned people versus the light-skinned people." What did she mean? Where had she gotten that? How do I tell her about racism without her jumping to being racist? I knew that she was confused about what she was learning in religious education—some of it was going over her head and some of it wasn't making sense to her, and it was uncomfortable to have to be in the position of explaining this before I felt like she was ready.

But this is just the age when she is ready. Another professor, Rebecca Bigler, did a study in which she took three preschool classes of four and five-year-olds, and she gave them t-shirts—half got red t-shirts and half got blue. They wore these t-shirts for several weeks. There were no other reinforcements of the shirt colors, unlike the brown-eyes/blue-eyes experiment. The teachers didn't mention them. Here's what Bronson and Merryman report:

> When asked which color team was better to belong to, or which team might win a race, they chose their own color. They liked the kids in their own group more and believed they were smarter than the other color. "The Reds never showed hatred for Blues," Bigler observed. "It was more like, 'Blues are fine, but not as good as us.'" When Reds were asked how many Reds were nice, they'd answer "All of us." Asked how many Blues were nice, they'd answer "Some." Some of the Blues were mean, and some were dumb—but not the Reds.[102]

Bigler's argument is that children are naturally prone to discrimination. Given nothing else to discriminate on, these children naturally started discriminating on the basis of shirt color. I've watched this happen with my own child. The first day of her ballet class, when she was four, she walked in and there was one other little girl who was wearing the exact same leotard as she was. Guess who she walked right up to and started making friends with? The one girl who she saw instantly that she had something in common with. Bronson and Merryman write:

> We might imagine we're creating color-blind environments for children, but differences in skin color or hair or weight are like differences in gender—they're plainly visible. We don't have to label them for them to become salient. Even if no teacher or parent mentions race, kids will use skin color on their own, the same way they use T-shirt colors.[103]

Given that race is a salient feature, and children will naturally start to discriminate on it, it is important for us, as individual parents and grandparents, and as a church, which is a learning and teaching institution, to have positive conversations about race wherein we teach our children about not just anti-racism but pro-diversity.

They will learn some things in school, of course. When we were in the car the other day, I told my daughter that there was no school on Monday. "Martin Luther King Jr. Day!" she said automatically, "I know, Mom." "Really?" I asked, "You've been talking about Martin Luther King, Jr. at school?" "We just read a whole book." I then asked her about Martin Luther King, Jr., and when she said he talked to a lot of people, I asked why, and we talked about King until we got to the issues of fairness and equality.

We had another opportunity to have one of these conversations when we went to the Henry Ford Museum over the holidays. I had forgotten that the Henry Ford Museum has Rosa Park's bus. Naturally, we went and saw the bus, and we talked a lot about it. I'm pleased that a couple of weeks later, when I ask my daughter who Rosa Parks was and what she did, she still remembered that she was told to move to the back of the bus, and she didn't, and they took her away to jail. She doesn't understand all the particulars yet, but she's got the basic story down.

The really good news is that this is something we've been talking about here, in our children's religious education classes. It may have made me uncomfortable to have my daughter raise these issues with me, but I'm very glad that she did. Sure there were issues with the curriculum being a little over her head, but overall it is better that we're raising these issues than that we're not. Our children need to start talking about these subjects as early as possible, while their minds are still open.

To go back to that old "Brown Eyes Blue Eyes" experiment, and "You have to be carefully taught," the point of that exercise wasn't a teacher trying to prove you could turn children into little racists by teaching them prejudice and discrimination. The point of that exercise was that she wanted to teach her children not to discriminate. She made the decision to teach this exercise the night Martin Luther King, Jr. was killed. She had been teaching her students about Martin Luther King, Jr., and she knew she had to do something, and she went in the next day and did the brown eyes/blue eyes exercise. Perhaps not surprisingly, years later, that exercise had stuck with that classroom's students. PBS's Frontline did a program with the class 14 years later, in the mid-eighties. Those third graders, now grown, were all vocal in their expressions of non-discrimination, standing up to friends and family against prejudice, even while still living in the same largely white, all Christian, conservative, small-town farming community.

That's what we have to be carefully taught, we've learned. We have to be carefully taught *not* to hate all the people our relatives hate. We have to be carefully taught to embrace diversity and multiculturalism. We have to be carefully taught.

How Healthcare Is Our Moral Issue

September 27, 2009
Universalist Unitarian Church of East Liberty
Clarklake, MI

In the eight years I've been in ministry, there have been a handful of national issues that have seemed to me to demand a loud, clear, moral voice from the faith community. I felt the need to speak up about the violence and discrimination I saw against the Muslim community following September 11th, 2001. I felt the need to talk about and organize forums in opposition to our going to war in Iraq. I mourned the victims of Hurricane Katrina and the seemingly overwhelming racism revealed in its aftermath. There are all sorts of moral outrages—threats to the environment, racism, heterosexism, classism, and all sorts of other evils—to confront in our society, but these national-level issues took a demanding center stage in their time, commanded my attention, and absorbed my thoughts for months. Now, the issue before us is health care reform.

While I also feel passionately about the other issues I've talked about—war and peace, racism, and religious equality—the moral issues around health care reform are personal to me in a way the others are not. Accordingly, it is difficult to preach about, because I not only care about it deeply and am angry on a sort of societal outrage level, I also have personal anger about it that is hard to set aside. In fact, I'm not entirely sure I want to. Striking the balance, though, is hard. It is by far harder to preach about the things that I am most passionate about and emotionally and deeply tied to, than it is about issues I can stand back from and know that my moral clarity is unbiased by my personal desires.

My own feelings stem from two incidents, which I will briefly relate. In 1993 I fell and broke my back, literally—my first lumbar vertebra (the lower back). I feel it today. I feel it every day when I stand up and preach. When I fell, I was uninsured, and I was working full-time for a healthcare company—Blue Care Network, an affiliated HMO of Blue Cross, Blue Shield. As a result of the fall, I lost my job, I lost my apartment, and I spent years paying off my medical debt, even after government assistance. I saw exactly what still remains after the government steps in and pays hospital bills, and you still have doctor's bills, ambulance bills, medications, and other things left to pay for.

The second incident was when I was moving here, and trying to find insurance that would cover me with a major pre-existing condition: a pregnancy. Only one insurance agency had to take me, Blue Cross, Blue Shield (my old nemesis). Furthermore, they didn't have to take my pre-existing condition of being pregnant, under most situations. It took several people working constantly on this situation for months to find me the loophole under which they had to cover my pregnancy—and thank goodness for them.

That, in a nutshell, has made me pretty seriously personally frustrated with the insurance system in the United States of America. I believe it needs major reform. I believe that the system is terribly broken.

But the case I want to make to you isn't about my personal experience. Furthermore, this is not about a public option. This is not about socialism. This is not an argument for abortion services to be covered. This is not about whether or not there are death panels. This is not about economics and what our country can afford. This is not about rationing. This is not an argument about a single-payer system. This is not an argument about problems in the insurance industry. This is not about Glenn Beck, Sean Hannity, or Rush Limbaugh. This is not a sermon about Republicans versus Democrats. This is not a sermon about House bills and Senate bills. This is not a sermon about racism against our president. (I do have strong opinions about all these things, of course.)

This is about a universal moral code. This is about the bottom line of what it means to be religious. This is about morality. What I want you to see is what is moral here. We're talking about this because it is a question of what is morally right. We're talking about moral imperatives.

Now, there are a lot of differences people hold on what is a moral imperative. For example, I found one quote from Michael Hlinka, a CBC business columnist, wherein he says, "I'm not about to knock anyone for getting as much as they can. That's something close to a moral imperative in my book."[104] Perhaps most of us would disagree, and say that the drive to get what you want is *not* a moral imperative. On the other hand, there's President Obama, who said, "We also need to provide Americans who can't afford health insurance more affordable options. That's an economic imperative, but it is also a moral imperative."[105] Here, I happen to agree. I see affordable health insurance as a moral imperative for our country. Now, Obama actually goes on to explain the reasons it is an economic imperative, but he doesn't really explain why it is a moral imperative. That remains, therefore, to be done here and now.

There are many sources of authority we could choose from, as Unitarian Universalists, to appeal to our moral consciousness. The Golden Rule exists in every major religion—that which tells us to treat others with the type of care that we wish to be treated with ourselves. Turning to the Bible, one of the first stories we get is the story of Cain and Abel, wherein Cain asks God, "Am I my brother's keeper?" Of course the reason why this piece of dialogue is such a famous line, the reason why it is repeated so many times, is because of course we are meant to understand that yes, we are our brother's keeper. That is to say, we are told we should respect all people, and care for them like our brothers. Then, in the gospels, with Jesus, we get his teachings. I believe that the meaning of being Christian isn't really about whether or not you believe Jesus was God, or whether or not he died on the cross, but whether you strive to live by his teachings, whether or not you choose to use Jesus and his message as a rubric for life. Jesus said, of course, telling about the kingdom of God in Matthew 25 (KJV):

> Then shall the King say unto them on his right hand, Come, ye blessed of my Father, inherit the kingdom prepared for you from the foundation of the world: For I was hungered, and ye gave me meat: I was thirsty, and ye gave me drink: I was a stranger, and ye took me in: Naked, and ye clothed me: I was sick, and ye visited me: I was in prison, and ye came unto me. Then shall the righteous answer him, saying, Lord, when saw we thee hungered, and fed thee? or thirsty, and gave thee drink? When saw we thee a stranger, and took thee in? or naked, and clothed thee? Or when saw we thee sick, or in prison, and came unto thee? And the King shall answer and say unto them, Verily I say unto you, inasmuch as ye have done it unto one of the least of these my brethren, ye have done it unto me.

If you think, well, Jesus just talks about visiting sick people, think about the medical knowledge of the time. Visiting a sick person then was pretty risky—you didn't know that you wouldn't be contaminated and die. Jesus asks people to risk their lives to take care of the sick. That's a whole lot more risky than anything we're being asked today to do to care for the sick. Furthermore, of course, many of Jesus' miracles have to do with healing, most famously raising Lazarus up from the dead, but in over twenty other accounts in the New Testament he heals the sick. If you look at all the miracles credited to Jesus, about 70 percent of them are healing, even if you count groups of people being healed as one miracle. (I'm also counting raising the dead and exorcisms as healing.) But this is pretty much all he does, other than turning water into wine one time and cursing a fig tree. Basically, this is what Jesus does during his life: He wanders around, gives lectures, and performs miracles, and the miracles he performs are almost always healing the sick. Likewise, the lectures he gives often talk about how we treat other people.

To be a Christian, you must follow Jesus' teachings. Jesus taught by his words and his actions, too. We can't perform miracles, but we can do everything we can to heal the sick. That includes giving them access to medical care.

But, as I said, in every other major religion, there is the Golden Rule, and every religion has stories that tell of the importance of healing the sick. We see in Buddhism, for example, that the entire religion is a response to suffering. Let me say that again: The *entire religion* is a response to suffering. The Buddha became the Buddha in response to the suffering he saw in the world. He was a prince, a man who himself had been protected. He had the Cadillac of health insurance of his day: His father kept anyone sick or dying from coming near his son. Then one day he goes out into the world and sees that not everybody has access to the life he leads, and he is overcome from this experience. He looks for answers to this, and he comes up with what we know as Buddhism.

I think you can look at the story of these two great teachers, Jesus and Buddha, as a story of two men who understood at the deepest level their moral obligations to others, and that those moral obligations were to alleviate suffering however possible. Jesus does it with miracles. Buddha does it with giving us the wheel of the law. We have equal moral obligation to the weight these two incredible men felt on their shoulders. We have a moral obligation to alleviate suffering. As religious people, we must look out into the world like Jesus and Buddha, and look for how we can alleviate suffering. Frankly, we can do it and must do it in this country. We don't need miracles; we don't have access to miraculous powers to heal the sick. However, we can do a lot more than we're doing now. We have amazing scientific knowledge that Jesus and Buddha didn't have access to. We have amazing medical practitioners. We can and must, as religious people, choose to heal the sick.

If we are moral, religious people, we must live up to this greatest moral imperative, this greatest moral obligation. Jesus saw suffering, and he went out and did something about it. Buddha saw suffering and he went out and did something about it. Yet now we have people in this country who dare to say that they are Christian, and they believe that the problem with health care reform is that we might possibility provide health care to immigrants? What would Jesus say about that? Oh, sorry, you're a Samaritan, not a Jew, and so I don't think you should have access to my miracles? No health care for illegal immigrants, they say, and then turn around and say this is a Christian nation? As long as anyone is turned away from medical treatment, there is no way that this is a Christian nation. If you believe that being Christian means being good, we are failing miserably.

Now, I know not everyone here wants to consider this a Christian nation. Perhaps you don't want to consider us a religious nation, either, because of separation of church and state. Regardless, I do want to consider us moral people. If you are a Christian person, or a religious person, or a moral person, our obligation is to care for others, not just ourselves. That's the essence of faith—this connection to something other than the selfish "I," the individual ego, that our greedy society would otherwise hold as primary. Furthermore, if we are a Christian country or a religious country or a moral country, we must show it in our actions of how we treat the poorest among us—and by saying it is about how we treat them, yes I mean it is how we treat them medically, as well. That is the essence of religion. If you have a connection to the divine, you have a connection to other people. Yet in this country we have people dying because they can't afford treatments. We have people becoming homeless because they can't pay their medical bills. We have people suffering because we horde health like it is a scarce resource. Meanwhile, we say we respect every person on the web of life in Unitarian Universalism, and we say in the United States of America everyone is created equal—and it is meaningless. This is an outrage. It is shameful. It is a failure of epic proportions.

If we are people of faith, if we are people who believe in our country, we have two choices: We can change this system, or we can live in shame, knowing that we saw the shining possibility of a truly great nation on a hill and we ran the other way out of selfishness, greed and fear.

I'm sorry if you want a nuanced approach today, full of openness and seeing all sides. I don't see it that way. There is love, and then there is this, the system that we have. There is living our religion, and then there is this, the system that we have. There is God's vision, and then there is the system that we have. We have a choice. We choose the path of love, of living our religion, of God's vision, or we choose the system that we have. There is no gray area to me. There is no time for a nuanced moderate approach. There are people dying out there, and we need to stop being the country that is killing them.

Becoming America:
Immigration

September 19, 2010
Universalist Unitarian Church of East Liberty
Clarklake, MI

There are a million immigration sermons to give, and hours, weeks, months, worth of data and arguments to sift through.

There's the economic argument: Are illegal immigrants harming our economy by taking our jobs? Well, a recent article in *Slate*, summing up some economists' arguments says no, immigrants "do not displace American workers."[106]

There's the peace and security argument: Are illegal immigrants bringing crime with them? Nobody debates that there are major drug problems going on in Mexico. However, a 2008 *Time* article said, "Immigrants in California are, in fact, far less likely than U.S.-born Californians are to commit crime. While people born abroad make up about 35% of California's adult population, they account for only about 17% of the adult prison population." More recent articles have pointed to similar statistics.

What about the "anchor baby" concept—the idea that women come here illegal to have their babies born as U.S. citizens to gain a foothold towards citizenship? People are now arguing for a rewrite of the 14th Amendment of the U.S. Constitution based on this one. Well, the facts are that a U.S.-born baby won't be able to help a parent stay in the U.S. for 21 years, so that's a longer wait than lots of other ways to get a foothold towards citizenship. It is indeed common for immigrants to have babies once there here because, well, it is very common for all types of people to make babies.

The arguments about immigration go on and on—fear that we'll become an entirely Spanish-speaking country, for example. Turns out that most publicly-funded English classes have wait lists, and then there are problems with being able to take English classes, such as changing work schedules or lack of childcare.[107] In fact, people are trying to learn English, and in many areas, as many people are learning English as we're providing resources for. Personally, I have no fear of the

United States of America becoming a Spanish-speaking country. We've been assimilating immigrants from other cultures for centuries here, and English has still predominated, as has what we think of as U.S. American culture. But if it were to happen in my lifetime that English became a minority language here and Spanish became the majority, well, then, I'd learn Spanish. That wouldn't be the end of the world. It would be good for me to learn Spanish. What's important about the United States of America to me is not our language or even our culture, but our ideals of democracy and freedom and equality. I have yet to meet or see on TV an illegal immigrant or a legal one who says, "I don't want to learn English or know anything about the United States of America; I just want to be here." I would guess that virtually 100% of illegal immigrants who don't speak English at all or well in this country wish they had better English, and if they had the time and money and aceess, and security to know they wouldn't be deported, they would like to learn English. Knowing English opens up opportunities, and they know this. However, it is not an easy language to learn, sometimes it is low on priorities when it is not seen as necessary in immigrant enclaves, and there are many barriers, such as fear of being deported, that prohibit many from taking English classes. In spite of this, the constant myth that immigrants don't *want* to learn English persists. It is a myth based in fear and prejudice. However, if there's a *fear* that the United States of America will turn Spanish, then there are two ways of responding that seem reasonable: teach more English to those who don't know it, or teach more Spanish to those who don't know it.

We could talk about the history of immigration in this country, how we've invited immigrant groups in to accomplish certain tasks, and then sent them packing again. We could talk about how recently immigration law really became part of the fabric of our society. We could talk about still pending legislation, like the DREAM Act, which will allow children who've lived the majority of their lives here to become citizens. We could talk about colonization and how we're all immigrants, and that the only people who are natives of this country are the Native Americans. We could talk about the border with Mexico and Westward Expansion, and how we took parts of the country away from Mexico and then separated families in the process. We could talk about how the drug cartels there are fueled by U.S. American drug use. I could review the work of the Unitarian Universalist Association campaign, Standing on the Side of Love. We could talk about the situation in Arizona, or the situation in Michigan. We could talk about the long list of pro-immigrants' rights social action statements we've passed as an association from 1961, the year we became the Unitarian Universalist Association, right up through the 2010 General Assembly, where we passed a business resolution, an action of immediate witness, and a study/action issue all related to immigration. Here's a sampling of things we've said as an association:

- 1963 General Resolution on Immigration: calls for an update to federal immigration policy, including to "remove the purely arbitrary barriers to immigration on the basis of race and national origin."
- 1995 Resolution of Immediate Witness to Call for Conscious, Humane Treatment of Immigrants: "demands a just application of human rights at both the state and national levels for all people living within our borders."
- 2006 Action of Immediate Witness to Support Immigrant Justice: calls for "just and comprehensive immigration reform."
- 2007 Action of Immediate Witness to Support Immigrant Families and Stop ICE Raids: calls for "an immediate moratorium of all inhumane raids and resulting deportations."

We could talk about how very difficult it is to come here legally. If you're not married to, or a minor child of, a citizen, and if you're not highly skilled and/or college educated, well, it doesn't matter how long you're willing to wait in line, it is not a matter of waiting in line—we don't have a slot that we're going to give to you.

We could talk about how our economic system relies on underpaid immigrant labor, and how that drives down the costs of our food and our goods. The Unitarian Universalist Association's study/action resources on immigration state:

The U.S. is dependant upon cheap labor to produce our fruits and vegetables, our meats, our clothing, and a myriad of other things. Manufacturers are dependent upon cheap labor to keep costs down and thus remain competitive in the marketplace. Consumers are dependent upon cheap products as the result of a combination of consumer mentality and a real decline in purchasing power for many of us. The result is a vicious downward spiral that exploits both undocumented workers and U.S. workers alike.[108]

Then, finally, there's the fall-back argument: Well, they're here illegally. Illegal immigration is illegal. They made a choice to do something illegal, and there should be consequences. End of story. But is it? We know from the stories of immigrant children that coming here illegally isn't always a choice one makes—in the case of children, it is a choice made for you. I've been learning, as well, that it is wrong to call someone an illegal immigrant. They're an undocumented immigrant. A person's being isn't illegal—what is illegal is an action a person takes. As the Holocaust survivor Elie Wiesel said:

You who are so-called illegal aliens must know that no human being is "illegal." That is a contradiction in terms. Human beings can be beautiful or more beautiful, they can be fat or skinny, they can be right or wrong, but illegal? How can a human being be illegal?[109]

This point may seem like semantics, but it is actually an important distinction, because by the very term "illegal immigrant" we are stripping their personhood of dignity. We are dehumanizing them with the term. The term "illegal immigrant" goes against one of the core principles of our faith: belief in the inherent worth and dignity of every human being.

What is usually illegal in the case of undocumented immigrants is not their personhood, it is how they got here—not going through a point of entry and being properly processed—or the fact that they stayed here in the case of those who overstayed their visas. The term "illegal," while technically appropriate, is often used along with calling undocumented immigrants "criminals," which is not the case. Undocumented immigrants have broken a civil code, not a criminal one.

We could talk about a million different aspects of the immigration debate, all of them worthy. What I most want to talk about, though, is love, compassion, and opening our hearts. Because that's what this is all about. What we do in our society, in all societies, is we learn to create "in" groups and "out" groups, and make the "out" groups the "other" and then convince ourselves that they, the "other," don't deserve ethical treatment, or they don't deserve what we have. The Nazis did this in Germany—convinced a people that the Jews were dirty, and greedy, and responsible for all their problems. We did this with Africans, and allowed ourselves to enslave them, because we were convinced they were lesser. In our society now, we do it with gays and lesbians, we do it with Muslims, we do it with undocumented immigrants.

We convince ourselves that we who were here when we got here have a right to be here, and those arrive after us don't have a right to be here. However, these borders are our own constructs—they are not God's and they are not nature's. We come here, we put a line, and we say you can't come here now that we're here, and then we convince ourselves that we're better in some way and more deserving of being here. We were born *here*. We know the language of *here*. Those people weren't *here* when we got here.

I didn't want to care about immigration. I had enough issues to care about. It wasn't my issue. I can trace my father's Landrum line back for nine generations and other lines eleven generations to when my family came into this country in 1688. The most recent immigrant in my family was four generations back on my mother's mother's side—so nobody within living memory.

But I started opening my heart when I heard stories like this one from a young man, Ivan Nikolav, who was raised in Michigan and missed one court date when he was 12. He was in detention for months when he wrote to the president saying:

> I immigrated to the United States from Russia when I was just 11 years old. My mother married a U.S. citizen who is the only father I know.... This is the only country I know as my home and I don't know what I would do if I were deported, now.
>
> I am a long-time resident of Michigan. I have a fiancée who has been with me for over three years....
>
> In Russia, it would be difficult for me to survive. I barely speak the language and I have very little family there.[110]

Ivan was released, thanks in large part to the Michigan activists who got his story out, but there are lots of stories like Ivan's. This is the first step—hearing stories of people like us, who were raised in the United States of America, graduated from U.S. high schools, maybe played sports or were honors students or went to their proms just like some of us, and who are actually undocumented immigrants. Once we can open our hearts here, just a crack, we start to let the barriers between "self" and "other" come down.

We should also consider stories of people like Jose Franco, who was going to come to the forum hosted by the Universalist Unitarian Church of East Liberty and speak, a courageous thing for an undocumented student to do. He wasn't able to come because he needed to go to Washington, D.C. and lobby for the DREAM Act. I share his name and story because he's brave enough to share it publically. Jose is 22 and came here at the age of 2. He says:

> I didn't know I was undocumented until I started elementary school, and I didn't really know what that meant until I went to high school and I noticed that a lot of people were dropping out because of legal status. They didn't believe that continuing on to higher education would matter to them...And that's how I felt.... I started skipping school.... But at one point I found out about this bill that would change everything that's called the DREAM Act which would give students like me who have been here since we were young...our legal status.[111]

Jose was arrested while protesting in D.C., something he risked everything to do. (He was released and his court date is still pending.)

If we let these stories open our hearts, then there's hope. It is imperative that we do this—we are compelled to do this work of opening our hearts and standing on the side of love. We have to do so because this is the universal religious impulse in which we believe. Every religion in the world tells us about love, and about how to treat our neighbor. This is the Golden Rule—the greatest task, the strongest commandment, the purpose of all the institutions we build and the work we do.

It all comes down to that: Love your neighbor. Who is your neighbor? When Jesus was asked that, he told the story of the Good Samaritan—a story of an outsider, someone from a group that was despised, who turned out to be the true neighbor. Who is our neighbor? Mexico is our neighbor.

Jesus is also reported to have said, "In God's love there is no Jew or Gentile." He sat and ate with lepers, and he said that God will welcome into Heaven those to whom God can say, "I was hungry and you gave me food, I was thirsty and you gave me drink, I was a stranger and you took me in." What, then, I ask you, is the Christian thing to do in response to illegal immigration? The Bible tells us that the answer is simple: offer sanctuary.

In the Biblical world, a sacred rule prescribed the way to treat strangers: One must treat strangers as one's guests by offering hospitality and protection. That's why Lot, in response to the angry mob demanding he send out the angels he has offered shelter to, offers to hand over his daughters instead. While the story also shows the sexism of the times, the story of Lot offering his daughters to satisfy an angry mob in order to protect his visitors is a story about how to treat strangers. That's what the story of Sodom and Gomorrah is about. To say it is about homosexuality is subterfuge. The story is a lesson on how we should treat our visitors, including immigrants—by welcoming them.

There are a lot of people who are motivated out of fear, or economic concern, or sometimes racism or xenophobia, and also out of places of ignorance, which leads them to a draconian view of immigration. I can understand how some can arrive at a strong stance against illegal immigration even from fairly positive motivations—national pride, fiscal conservatism, belief in strong law enforcement and belief in following rules. But what bothers me is when people try to say their anti-immigration stance is a religious one, or that it is what the United States of America stands for.

The United States of America, friends, is the land of opportunity—the land where we lift our lamp beside our door and welcome in the huddled masses yearning to be free. The United States of America is the melting pot, where people of all cultures come together. That's the United States of America I value and want to keep. How do we keep this vision of the United States of America? We keep it, now that we've done what we've done and taken this land from the Native Americans, by keeping our ideas—by extending them out and welcoming in.

What is religion about? Christianity is about love thy neighbor, Judaism about the Exodus story of coming to a new land, Unitarian Universalism about Standing on the Side of Love. Religion has a real clear answer to immigration, and like many answers religion has, our secular society doesn't want to hear it. Religion fights for justice and opportunity and freedom. Period. No exclusions, no caveats, no whining that I was here first and if I share what I have I'll have less. It may be a harsh discipline to stand for, and I understand that people can't always live up to the extremes of their values. However, these values are here to inspire us, to call us, to demand that we try everything we can to be the best U.S. Americans we can be, the best people we can be, the best neighbors we can be—to achieve the shirt-off-our-backs, borders down, other-cheek-turned, opened-door society that is the beloved kingdom here on earth. This society we live in may never get there, but by God, that's what we strive for in this faith.

May it be so.

Same-Sex Marriage

February 4, 2004
Fitchburg Sentinel & Enterprise

Last summer I performed a marriage ceremony for one of the most special and deeply-in-love couples I've had the privilege to meet. Their ceremony, with family and friends present, was simple and heart-felt, reflecting family traditions of both sides, with a gentle humor and a steadfast certainty. Afterwards, I signed a document and handed it to the couple with the certainty that this document would provide them with...absolutely nothing. Because they were both female, their marriage, seen as real in their eyes, my eyes, the eyes of their family and friends, and the eyes of God, would not be a marriage in the eyes of Massachusetts.

It was partly because of that experience that a few months ago I signed a document stating that I would not sign marriage licenses until the state legalized same-sex marriage. I did this because there is a distinction between civil marriage and religious marriage, and while I, as a religious official, will perform religious ceremonies for both heterosexual and same-sex couples, I could no longer, in good conscience, be an agent of a state that discriminates.

On Wednesday, the Massachusetts Supreme Judicial Court affirmed their earlier decision on the Goodridge case by stating that the only thing that will uphold equality for same-sex couples in the Commonwealth under the constitution is marriage, not civil unions. This is twice now that the court has explained that separate is not equal, and that same-sex marriage is an issue of civil rights. Taking this to a vote of all the citizens of the state would not answer the basic question of what is right and what is wrong—only what is most popular. Civil rights have always been about protecting the minority from the majority. Ultimately, this issue comes down to fairness and equality versus protecting the status quo.

Several arguments have been put forth against same-sex marriage. The first is by religious organizations who argue that God's message forbids same-sex marriage. Whose God is this? The God I could believe in upholds love and justice, not hatred or bigotry. God is in favor of family values—values that uphold and support families like love and justice and peace—and that includes families headed by same-sex couples. Furthermore, in a nation that believes in separation of church and state, and which holds a diversity of religions within its borders, to argue for state policy on the basis of religious beliefs is to undermine what makes our country strong.

This leads us to a second common argument against same-sex marriage: Legalizing it requires religious officials to perform ceremonies against their religious beliefs. This is blatantly false. Here, a distinction between civil and religious marriage becomes important. State-sanctioned marriage for same-sex couples will not make any religion or religious official required to perform any ceremony against their religious beliefs. Just as any religious official can currently refuse to perform a ceremony for a couple who comes from different religious backgrounds, any religious official or organization can make their own decisions regarding same-sex couples. Civil marriage means only that the government is required to treat all couples alike.

Same-sex marriage is something I have a religious belief in. Paradoxically, I could argue that my rights as a religious official are being violated—my right to practice my religious beliefs by providing marriage for same-sex couples has been infringed upon since the state has previously refused to recognize the ceremonies I perform with the same legitimacy that it gives to heterosexual unions. Marriage is an ancient institution, and religious marriage existed long before civil marriage. One could argue that the state ought to stay out of the marriage business altogether to avoid religious bias, or to simply ratify whatever a recognized religion performs, and because of the conflation of religious and civil marriage, this has validity. However, civil marriage is necessary for other reasons—to simplify our laws of inheritance, parental rights and responsibilities, insurance, taxation, immigration, next-of-kin rights, and the 1400 rights and privileges that are attached to civil marriage in our state. While religious marriage may be what joins a couple in the eyes of God or the eyes of community, family, and friends, it is also a license that binds all the rest of these rights and privileges to this institution of marriage.

When we think about what marriage is about, our first answer is love. Same-sex couples have plenty of love. It is not the place of the state to judge love. Nor is that the purpose of civil marriage. As long as rights and privileges are attached to this institution by the state, all couples deserve access to that license.

Another argument against same-sex marriage is that it will weaken the institution of marriage. At this point, my husband often asks me, "Honey, will same-sex couples marrying weaken our marriage?" The answer, of course, is that such a thought is ridiculous. To the contrary, supporting the love of couples who want to make a lifetime commitment to each other can only strengthen the institution of marriage. What marriage, as an institution needs, is people who are committed to it entering into it. Actually, prohibiting same-sex marriage does not strengthen but rather weakens the institution, as it makes our country one of hypocrisy.

So, again I ask the question, "Will same-sex couples marrying weaken my marriage?" The answer: not at all. But not allowing same-sex couples to marry weakens our nation, built upon the pillars of freedom, justice, and equality.

Standing on the Side of Love This Valentine's Day

February 10, 2010
Jackson Citizen Patriot

With Valentine's Day right around the corner, our thoughts naturally go to the subject of love. In celebration of love, many loving couples will make a legal commitment to each other. But there are a lot of loving couples in our community who cannot celebrate in this way because of our state's limitations on same-sex marriage. Many of the same-sex couples that I know are in relationships that have lasted longer than my marriage. These couples are raising children. They own houses together. They are an asset to our community. The same-sex couples I know have marriages that are every bit as real, loving, committed, and important as the marriages of the heterosexuals in our community. They are in every significant way like my husband and me, except under the law. There is in no way that these loving relationships threaten the institution of marriage. If marriage as an institution is threatened, it is by those who take it casually, which is done by heterosexuals all the time. None of the same-sex couples I know take the issue of marriage casually at all.

The majority of U.S. Americans now believe in "civil unions," and are willing to give same-sex couples the same rights that we give to heterosexual couples. For some, however, the sticking point comes with not wanting to call a civil union "marriage." Civil marriage, however, is a civil right. If we conferred the same rights to civil unions that we give to civil marriages, then this civil right would be met, and the difference in the name "union" versus "marriage" would be semantic only. But with differing state and international laws, creating a category of "union" that is equivalent to "marriage" is impossible.

In many countries, civil marriage and religious marriage are distinctly separate. It is because of our blending of the two that this is such a contentious issue. For example, as a minister, I perform a state function when I sign marriage licenses. In many other countries, religious ceremonies have no legal function. Religious marriage, on the other hand, is a sacrament of the church or other religious institution. Since we have separation of church and state, religious beliefs should have no bearing on civil marriage and vice versa. People often mistakenly believe that if we legalize civil marriage for same-sex couples, then ministers who object will be forced to perform those marriages. This is simply not true.

A minister can refuse to perform any marriage, for any reason, particularly when he or she has religious objections. Several years ago, when I was a minister in Massachusetts, I signed a vow saying that I wouldn't sign any marriage licenses until the state allowed me to sign them for same-sex couples as well. Happily, I was able to sign some of those licenses before I left the state to come home to Michigan.

I would expect that if same-sex marriages were legalized, many ministers might similarly refuse to be agents of the state when they believe the state's actions are wrong. This is one of the privileges of freedom of religion, and I respect the right to not perform same-sex marriage. Likewise, I am proud to stand on the side of love on this issue and perform same-sex marriages in our community, whether the state recognizes them or not.

Marriage is a bond of love, a sacred trust between two people. Any couple able to make this commitment to each other and take this vow seriously deserves the legal benefits of marriage. As a community and state, we need to stand on the side of love.

Of Love and Marriage

February 22-23, 2003
The Gardner News

When I was just starting out in ministry, I met a lesbian couple who asked me to perform their wedding service, or service of union. This was the first time I had ever been asked as a minister to perform a service for gay or lesbian people. I agreed to do it, and set a meeting.

They had wanted to get married in Hawaii, which had more liberal laws for gay and lesbian people than the state we were living in, but one of them had just started a new job and couldn't get the necessary time off. Their trip had to be called off at the last minute, yet still wanting to get married on the same date, they had anxiously started calling ministers in the yellow pages.

Neither of the women had rented a hall or a church, so they asked me where the ceremony should be. Knowing finances were an issue, I suggested we meet in a public park, by a lake, and do the service outside. I had done a wedding there only a week before, and it had been a lovely location. They agreed, although hesitant about it being such a public location, because they didn't want anyone to come by and heckle them. One of the women also asked me what she should wear. I replied, hesitantly, "Well, I guess you should wear whatever you want to. Something a little dressy would probably be good."

When I got there, I found that only two other people were coming, as witnesses. The autumn day was colder than expected, and they were all shivering. I was shivering, too, even in my usually overly-warm preaching robe. The dark, too, fell faster than we thought it would, and by the end of the service I could barely read the page in front of me. We attempted to have a unity candle ceremony, but the candles kept blowing out in the wind. There was no music, no one to give either bride away, and as far as I knew, no reception afterwards. The few people, mostly joggers, who passed by on the trail took no notice of our little huddled group of people, even with me in my robe and stole.

It was, by far, one of the worst jobs I've ever done at performing a wedding—not because of elements I could control, but because of the overall atmosphere. I felt unsure of myself, knowing it was a new experience for me, and I wished I could have made things nicer for them.

But at the end of the ceremony, as we walked towards the parking lot, I saw that both brides had tears in their eyes. As we signed their certificate of union on the hood of their car, they each gave me hugs, thanked me, and told me how wonderful it was for them. Even in the cold and dark, the park had been a beautiful location with the lake in the background.

Years later, I received a letter from these two women—they were still together, and planning another larger and more formal ceremony to be held on their anniversary. That simple, quickly-planned, humble service had been a real wedding for them, one that endured, nurtured, and sustained them.

I learned something that day. I learned that a service of union can be different from a wedding in more ways than just the lack of a state seal. Their service was different because of the lack of support from family and friends and colleagues. It was different because even during one of their happiest moments, they still feared persecution. It was different because these two women, despite the depth and commitment of their love, knew that they could not share this happy event with colleagues when they went back to work on Monday.

With a deep religious conviction, I believe that this love should be celebrated, not persecuted, and that such a day will come. But until such a day comes, those of us who are on the side of love and not hate must continue on, doing what we can, supporting those we know, and loving. Above all, if God is love, God is smiling down on those two women today, as they rejoice in the love they share.

The Essence of Conscience: To Kill a Mockingbird

March 11, 2007
Universalist Unitarian Church of East Liberty
Clarklake, MI

Despite an undergraduate and graduate degree in English, I had never read *To Kill a Mockingbird*. Indeed, for much of my youth, I confused it with *One Flew Over the Cuckoo's Nest*, which I also hadn't read, simply because they both contained birds in their titles. For some reason, I had also never seen either of the movies of the books. So, while a certain amount of knowledge from popular culture had managed to invade my consciousness, when the Jackson, Michigan community started the Big Read, an NEA program wherein the whole community is encouraged to read the same book and attend programs relating to the book, I was able to come to the book with fresh eyes. It occurred to me as I was writing this sermon, and searching the web, that I was doing what countless numbers of high school students have done for decades. It is apparent just how widely read *To Kill a Mockingbird* is by the number of essays available on the internet for students to plagiarize. It is ironic that a book so about the conscience and justice, and indeed, the purpose of education, is probably one that inspires a great deal of plagiarism. It is also ironic that the book is so read at schools, as Scout is continually making arguments to her father Atticus about why she shouldn't have to go to school—when Atticus tells her not to use the n-word, she tells him she learned it at school, and if he doesn't want her to learn these things, maybe she shouldn't have to go.

There are so many themes in Harper Lee's classic novel, *To Kill a Mockingbird*, that are worthy of discussion. Indeed, there are many that fit tightly with our Unitarian Universalist Principles. I want to speak about a couple of them. First, I want to speak about the conscience, and secondly about hope and moving on in the face of the knowledge of evil.

One of our Unitarian Universalist Principles is the right of conscience and the respect of the democratic process—two things Atticus Finch stands up for like no one else in *Mockingbird*. Indeed, the town gives him the role of being the conscience for them all. Scout shows this to the mob at the jail through talking to Mr. Cunningham about how Atticus has helped him, and it turns the crowd around. Later, at the trial for Tom Robinson, Atticus describes all the ways people are not actually equal in this country, and then states:

> But there is one way in this country in which all men are created equal—there is one human institution that makes a pauper the equal of a Rockefeller, the stupid man the equal of an Einstein, and the ignorant man the equal of any college president. That institution, gentlemen, is a court. It can be the Supreme Court of the United States or the humblest J.P. court in the land, or this honorable court which you serve. Our courts have their faults, as does any human institution, but in this country our courts are the great levelers, and in our courts all men are created equal.

Of course, the jury does not live up to Atticus's impassioned speech about equality. In fact, even today, we still do not live up to that dream of justice and equality. We know that the death penalty is still given disproportionately to African-American men. Indeed, the justice system is not color blind, and we are systematically imprisoning the African-American population as we mete out injustice for many, not justice for all. The book *To Kill a Mockingbird* remains as horribly true and as horribly relevant as it did when it first appeared over thirty—close to forty years ago.

The second thing I wanted to talk about is despair, hope, and perseverance in the presence of an unreasonable and unjust world. In *To Kill a Mockingbird*, we have the example of a justice system where Atticus bravely and heroically fights the un-winnable case, as he says, "Simply because we're licked a hundred years before we started is no reason for us not to try to win." But Tom Robinson is found guilty anyway because in a place like Maycomb, Alabama, during the Great Depression, justice for any black man accused of raping a white woman was not possible to be found. And Tom Robinson despairs. Atticus says, "They shot him...He was running. It was during their exercise period. They said he just broke into a blind raving charge at the fence and started climbing over. Right in front of them.... The guards called to him to stop. They fired a few shots in the air, then to kill. They got him just as he went over the fence. They said if he'd had two good arms he'd have made it, he was moving that fast. Seventeen bullet holes in him. They didn't have to shoot him that much."

Tom looked at the situation facing him, and even though Atticus thought he had a good chance of winning the appeal, he couldn't take it. He gambled on the odds of a slight chance of escape against large odds of death, and he lost.

The book could leave us there, in that moment of despair, with the thought that it is a sin to kill a mockingbird. Aunt Alexandra says it is the last straw. Atticus seems to despair, as well. But the book doesn't begin and end in that moment. The message of the book is larger than the senselessness and the tragedy and the injustice. The book gives the hope for future justice, the hope that the world will change or is changing. Even after that, Atticus teaches love to Scout, rather than hate. She asks if it is okay to hate Hitler. "It is not," he said. "It's not okay to hate anybody."

Despite the tragedy that occurs, the messages that Atticus teaches his children throughout the book give a moral compass in this wilderness. Throughout the book, Scout learns the message that there is only one kind of person—not four as Jem suggests, not even two, but that everybody is the same. When Scout hears Atticus called by a dirty name, he says, "I do my best to love everybody." When Jem fights back against Mrs. Dubose after Mrs. Dubose makes disparaging statements, Atticus makes Jem read for Mrs. Dubose daily. After Mrs. Dubose's death, Atticus says:

> I wanted you to see something about her—I wanted you to see what real courage is, instead of getting the idea that courage is a man with a gun in his hand. It's when you know you're licked before you begin but you begin anyway and you see it through no matter what. You rarely win, but sometimes you do. Mrs. Dubose won, all ninety-eight pounds of her. According to her views, she died beholden to nothing and nobody. She was the bravest person I ever knew.

After the case is lost, and also after Tom's death, Jem gets very moody. He is disillusioned in a system that he thought was shining and good, and it gives him great despair. However, in Boo Radley we find hope after all that despair. Tom is one Mockingbird who is dead. When Boo kills a man, the main characters realize he's the Mockingbird who it would be a sin to kill. There is progress, in some ways, in the fact that one death keeps another from happening. At the end of the book, Scout is able to take a figure that she had seen as a sort of boogeyman, and walk a mile in his shoes. She says, "Atticus was right. One time he said you never really know a man until you stand in his shoes and walk around in them. Just standing on the Radley porch was enough." Scout shows us that hope is there for the future—she can see through another's perspective, just as sees through Jem's despairing point of view that there are four types of people to realize that, in fact, there is only one.

In the beginning of the book, Scout and Jem have the faith of children in a universe that is benevolent. It is that trust in ultimate goodness that gives Scout the ability to turn back a mob of angry townspeople who have a showdown with

Atticus at the jail. The world Jem and Scout have experienced is good, and they have no understanding of evil. In the injustice done to Tom Robinson, and in the attack from Mr. Ewell, they experience the other side, and have to incorporate this into their worldview. But with the guiding figure of Atticus Finch, we are not left to believe that the world is purely a world of evil, purely of injustice. In spite of everything, he does not give up. Likewise, he will not let Scout or Jem give up, either. Atticus can defend Tom Robinson, knowing that he was bound to lose, and see the good in a jury that deliberates much longer than he expected. Atticus can also see the good in a racist neighbor, because of the level of courage she had in facing the pain in her life.

While the messages of the novel are so much in consonance with our principles—messages of integrity, justice, equality, anti-racism, anti-prejudice, tolerance, equity—what I find most remarkable today is the message of hope. Anne Frank said:

> It's difficult in times like these: ideals, dreams and cherished hopes rise within us, only to be crushed by grim reality. It's a wonder I haven't abandoned all my ideals, they seem so absurd and impractical. Yet I cling to them because I still believe, in spite of everything, that people are truly good at heart. I simply can't build my hopes on a foundation of confusion, misery, and death... and yet...I think...this cruelty will end, and that peace and tranquility will return again.

One might wonder how a story that ends in a tragic death like Anne Frank's could be a story of hope, but it, too, carries that message within it because of the spirit of the author. Harper Lee gives in the character of Scout the ability to live out that same sort of idealism in the face of this broken world she inherits. Upon hearing Jem's theory of brokenness, she offers up a vision of wholeness instead. It is a vision that I hope we embrace in our Unitarian Universalist churches and take out into the world.

The Grapes of Wrath in Our Time

March 15, 2009
Universalist Unitarian Church of East Liberty
Clarklake, MI

When opening up *The Grapes of Wrath* for the first time, the first thing that might hit someone is the overwhelming sorrow, even horror, of it. Early in the book, in one of the more expository chapters, Steinbeck writes:

> Some of the owner men were kind because they hated what they had to do, and some of them were angry because they hated to be cruel, and some of them were cold because they had long ago found that one could not be an owner unless one were cold. And all of them were caught in something larger than themselves. Some of them hated the mathematics that drove them, and some were afraid, and some worshipped the mathematics because it provided a refuge from thought and from feeling. If a bank or a finance company owned the land, the owner man said, The Bank—or the Company—needs—wants—insists—must have—as though the Bank or the Company were a monster, with thought and feeling, which had ensnared them.[112]

It is easy to take from this—and from the endless stories of people suffering, of children starving, of men desperate for work to support their families, of thousands homeless and living in cardboard boxes—only this message of anger, of wrath, of which Steinbeck writes:

> The people come with nets to fish for potatoes in the river, and the guards hold them back; they come in rattling cars to get the dumped oranges, but the kerosene is sprayed. And they stand still and watch the potatoes float by, listen to the screaming pigs being killed in a ditch and covered with quicklime, watch the mountains of oranges slop down to a putrefying ooze; and in the eyes of the people there is the failure; and in the eyes of the hungry there

is a growing wrath. In the souls of the people the grapes of wrath are filling and growing heavy, growing heavy for the vintage.[113]

Surely the title message is a strong message of the book, regarding the importance and value of anger in the face of this horror. It is a message that we can still use today, about the ways the systems allow us to turn aside from the humanity of others, to do things that are unconscionable and then blame them on the banks or the companies. We, too, have seen and are seeing homes foreclosed on in the same way. We are seeing what Steinbeck describes when he talks about the price of produce being driven down by the canneries to the point that farmers who don't own canneries can't afford a living. We are seeing what he describes—people working a full-time job yet still unable to pay for basic necessities. Sometimes we, too, turn the blind eye or, like the company and bank men he describes, blame it on the system in order to absolve our own responsibility to our brothers and sisters.

There is so much of this that we're feeling in our time, like the rage of seeing banks receiving bail-out money only to raise corporate executive salaries, while home after home forecloses because of the lack of a couple months of mortgage payments while the bread-winner was unemployed or incurring a rising medical debt. We see the outrages—different ones, on a different scale—like the hundreds of applications submitted for a minimum-wage job, where the applicants know that the waged earned won't cover their bills, but they have to try anyway. Also, yes, we see land lying fallow because farming it would cost more money than the harvested produce would be worth.

The backlash against Steinbeck was strong for *The Grapes of Wrath*. His book was banned—and burned. Numerous books were written in opposition to the work trying to show the more positive side of humanity—of the growers, owners and bankers, and their treatment of the displaced workers. One reason for the backlash was self-protection. But there's another reason, too, that we can relate to: one natural response to the anger—wrath—of the book, is to struggle against Steinbeck's claim of man's inhumanity to man with saying this is not the true nature of people, and people are naturally humane.

However, I think Steinbeck's message of struggle, of pain, is not the only message of the book. While a rain of plagues comes down on the Joad family and the other Okies, we see something in their struggle that is the larger message.

One message is in the religious themes of the book. One of the first comes from the character Rose of Sharon. When we first see her, this is the description: "Her whole thought and action were directed inward on the baby. She was balanced on her toes now, for the baby's sake. And the world was pregnant to her; she thought only in terms of reproduction and of motherhood."[114] In this description, we see a world of possibility, a world of hopefulness. We see also, a young woman who will change, over the course of the novel, from being inward-focused, to giving the final act of altruism in the end. We see a young woman who, over the course of the novel, tells the Christian story of Jesus from the woman's perspective. She is Mary, here, pregnant with the Christ-child, and at the end she forms a pietà, holding a dying man in her arms and giving him comfort. Rose of Sharon shows us the world of the human experience, from hope to loss, from inward-focused youth to the caring, giving mother she will become, even though she lost her child. The overall novel, too, gives us the story of Exodus as one of its other religious themes. We see when they arrive in California that the land looks like the Garden of Eden with its ripe fruit trees and lush terrain. The Christian themes abound in this novel, starting with the title, "Grapes of Wrath," which invokes "The Battle Hymn of the Republic," Julia Ward Howe's famous religious hymn:

> Mine eyes have seen the glory of the coming of the Lord:
> He is trampling out the vintage where the grapes of wrath are stored;
> He hath loosed the fateful lightning of His terrible swift sword:
> His truth is marching on.

Another religious element is the character of Casy. Casy is the preacher who Tom Joad first meets in the novel before meeting up with his family. Casy has given up preaching because he now sees everything as holy. He goes with them to wander in the wilderness, and then, in order to protect Tom Joad, is taken off to jail for a crime he didn't commit. Like Jesus, Casy is falsely restrained and punished by the authorities. When he gets out of jail, he leads a picket of workers against a farm trying to pay them less than they need to buy a day's food. Casy is killed for this resistance, finishing out his Christ allegory.

While all these Christian themes abound in the novel, however, they are not the major message I take from it. The main message I take from *The Grapes of Wrath* is a humanist one, which is why it works so well as a story for our faith. What I see in *The Grapes of Wrath* is, primarily, a novel about how people retain their humanity, a novel about our first principle of the inherent worth and dignity of every person. That's where people who want to deny the inhumanity presented in the book get the book wrong, because it fundamentally tells of the struggle to retain humanity in the face of opposition to it. We who have seen what the later world wrought, the genocide of the Holocaust and other subsequent genocides, for example, know that people can do horrible, horrific things to other humans. However, the novel gives us the other side, too, in the altruism of Rose of Sharon and in Casy and Tom's actions. The novel tells us of how, throughout all of the inhumane treatment, people can retain their human dignity and sense of worth.

Steinbeck clearly thinks that one way people retain their humanity is through wrath. He says:

> The women watched the men, watched to see whether the break had come at last…And where a number of men gathered together, the fear went from their faces, and anger took its place. And the women sighed with relief, for they knew it was all right—the break had not come; and the break would never come as long as fear could turn to wrath.[115]

Here's where the connection to Julia Ward Howe's song of anger and retribution for the crime of slavery becomes more palpable. The anger, the rage, the wrath is a wrath against crimes against humanity, against man's inhumanity to man; it is the rage proclaiming that despite whatever has been done to these people, they are still human, still have that inherent worth and dignity.

Yet anger is not the only way human dignity is proclaimed. Just as human dignity is shown through fire, it is shown through water; just as it is shown through men's wrath, it is shown through women as well. Ma Joad is the ultimate example of this. She says to Pa Joad, "Woman can change berr'n a man…Woman got all her life in her arms. Man got it all in his head. Don' you mind." He replies by listing off all their problems and saying, "Seems like our life's over an' done." Ma then says:

> It ain't, Pa. An' that's one more thing a woman knows. I noticed that. Man, he lives in jerks—baby born an' a man dies, an' that's a jerk—gets a farm an' loses his farm, an' that's a jerk. Woman, it's all one flow, like a stream, little eddies, little waterfalls, but the river it goes right on. Woman looks at it like that. We ain't gonna die out. People is goin' on—changin' a little, maybe, but goin' right on.[116]

That's what we see, if we look through the constant barrage of mistreatment and inhumanity thrown at the Joad family in *The Grapes of Wrath*; we see them responding with humanity. It is there the very first time they set camp along the highway, when they first ask the others camping if they may join them. They constantly do this, to the surprise of their fellow travelers, and it is a sign that they are treating each person they encounter with respect. When they meet another family with a run-down vehicle, they band together and help them out. When Ma Joad is cooking and a large group of little children gathers, she knows she doesn't have enough food for all of them, and she knows her own family is going hungrier than they should, yet she still can't help but give each child a taste. When the workers in the book are offered too little for their wages, they band together. At the end, when the Joads meet a man dying of starvation, the book ends on a message of self-sacrifice to help a stranger—the wounded traveler by the side of the road helped by the good Samaritan.

We learn through the novel that it is the people collectively, when working together, who will build up the treatment of others with human dignity and worth. We see it when the Joads live in the government camp, where the people rule themselves, and do so with dignity and honor. They build up their living conditions and their system of government in a way where everyone is included and made useful.

Casy also shows us the power of collective action through trying to explain the pickets to Tom. Tom doesn't immediately understand that it is something they must do, too. He is concerned with the immediate, with making money for the family and for food. But when Casy's predictions of wage cuts once the strike is broken come true, Tom quickly learns that the message here is a larger one, that his quest is a larger one. Tom summarizes Casy's explanation of scripture saying, "Two are better than one, because they have a good reward for their labor. For if they fall, the one will lif' up his fellow, but woe to him that is alone when he falleth, for he hath not another to help him up."[117] The message is clear: we must help our companions on this life's journey; it is in doing so that we are human.

Today, in our society, this is a message we're still learning. Tom quickly learns of the power of people united, of the unions, saying:

> "I been think' how it was in that gov'ment camp, how our folks took care a theirselves, an' if they was a fight they fixed it theirself; an' they wasn't no cops wagglin' their guns, but they was better order than them cops ever give. I been a-wonderin' why we can't do that all over. Throw out the cops that ain't our own people. All work together for our own thing—all farm our own lan'."[118]

In recent decades, we've seen the percentage of people in unions lessening, and the lack of understanding of the purpose and need for unions growing. I, personally, believe that our free faith understands that it takes "many drops to turn a mill," but we have grown increasingly ineffectual at articulating this to the larger society.

We have consistently heard the message in our news media for years that the answer is an American Dream of absolute capitalism and trickle-down economics—let people make of themselves what they may and pull themselves up by their bootstraps. Recently James Poniewozik wrote, "To watch CNBC today is to enter an alternative universe, where élites are populists, Wall Street is Main Street and bank executives are the oppressed."[119] How many times have we heard that it is the unions, demanding decent wages, that are responsible for everything from the struggle of the auto industry to the state of education? The voice against the common people banding together to improve their situation is stronger than ever, which is why Steinbeck's message still carries such an important message for our time. The answer may be in a return to wrath, or in a return to Ma Joad's message of the flow of the river as times move and change, but either way, the answer is in a return to examining situations in terms of people and lives, not numbers. We need more writers to call us to remember and honor humanity in times of great crisis. We are fortunate that we still have Steinbeck to call us to remember this message as well.

Poetic Calling: Arts of Ministry and Ars Poetica

October 2009
Ohio River Group

"Ars gratia artis" is the Latin for "Art for art's sake." When it comes to poetry, in relationship to my ministry, the art of poetry has many purposes beyond artistic merit. Poetry has been my scripture for many years, the text I turn to for inspiration in times of trouble, and in spiritual practice. Poetry has, therefore, a unique relationship to my ministry—one that is more than just the relationship of tool to wielder, and more than just artistic expression. In exploring just what poetry is to me as a minister, what purpose it serves in my ministry, I start with the fact that, for me, religious language and poetic language have a great deal of overlap. They are not necessarily one and the same, religious language and poetic language, but there is an intersection that is important and meaningful.

In her Berry Street Address of 2003, Unitarian Universalist minister Laurel Hallman writes:

> I believe that poetry is scripture. I believe that scripture is poetry. I believe that poetry is the way deep truth is transmitted person to person and generation to generation. I believe that when Emily Dickinson said, "Tell the truth/but tell it slant" she was speaking of metaphorical truth, the poetic truth that nourishes the heart, and opens the mind, and communicates to the depths. By poetry I mean the products of the religious imagination.[120]

Hallman speaks of scripture/poetry as addressing heart and mind, helping us with healing, connecting to the ultimate, and finding religious truth. These connect to several of the ways poetry functions as a scripture to me. Rita Dove, former poet laureate of the United States, addresses another function of scripture/poetry when she says, in response to Bill Moyers' question, "What does poetry have to say to power?": "By making us stop for a moment, poetry gives us an opportunity to think about ourselves as human beings on this planet and what we meant to each other."[121] Dove's description of the power of poetry is much like what one might give for a description of worship: the opportunity to stop and think about ourselves, our connections to others.

The poet Jane Hirschfield talks about the intersection of her practice of writing poetry and her practice of sitting zazen (sitting in Zen Buddhist meditation) in an article by Colleen Morton Busch. Busch writes:

> "Poems," she says, "are maps to the place where you already are." Zazen, she says, cultivates the ability to "stay open to what comes and *with* what comes," just as a poet's attention must do in receiving a poem from the imagination.... "When I sit zazen, I don't write poems," says Hirshfield, "I am entering a condition of concentration, of being with this moment as it is.... But in poetry, it's almost as if it is the same request made of my deep self, but with the intention pointed toward words rather than toward wordlessness."[122]

That phrase, "It is the same request made of my deep self," is, I believe, a phrase that describes both the essence of poetry and the essence of religious or spiritual practice. To put it in other words, Garrison Keillor writes in *Good Poems for Hard Times*, "What really matters about poetry and what distinguishes poets from, say, fashion models or ad salesmen is the miracle of incantation in rendering the gravity and grace and beauty of the ordinary world and thereby lending courage to strangers."[123]

Since poetic language and religious language have a great deal of overlap in form, meaning, and purpose, we can conclude that a possible explanation for this is that the role of the poet in our society has certain similarities to the role of the minister. We often speak of ministers as having many roles that begin with "P": preacher, prophet, pastor, priest. Ironically, we do not add: poet. However, the poet also functions in ways similar to many of these. Bill Moyers writes in his book, *The Language of Life: A Festival of Poets*, "Poetry is the most honest language I hear today...The poets I have met would be incapacitated if they did not write from a place of truth. Revelation is their reason for being."[124] Moyers' statement is very like the oft-repeated one of the role of the minister as "speaking truth to power." This is a role the poets also take up. Moyers continues:

> Revelation comes hard. As Stanley Kunitz once acknowledged, "...A word is a utilitarian tool to begin with, and we have to re-create it, to make it magical. You have to kill off all the top of one's head, remove it, and try to plunge deep into self, deep into memories, deep into the unconscious life. And then begin again."[125]

Kunitz uses very violent imagery, and that may perhaps block some from seeing how he is talking about spirituality, about the role of the poet to cut through everyday reality and go deep into the spiritual, but his image of removing the top of one's head is reminiscent of the imagery in a poem titled "Mother Wisdom Speaks," by Christine Lore Webber:

> Some of you I will hollow out.
> I will make you a cave.
> I will carve you so deep the stars will shine in your darkness.
> You will be a bowl.
> You will be the cup in the rock collecting rain...
> I will do this because the world needs the hollowness of you.[126]

Kunitz is speaking of himself as a poet and the spiritual practice and discipline needed for poetry, while Webber is speaking more generically about a spiritual calling and explaining it through poetry, but they both speak to the intersection of poet and minister.

This idea of the poet as minister is not a new one, certainly. It is been used by poets throughout the ages. For example, in an article about Elizabeth Barrett Browning, Karen Dieleman writes:

> In her correspondence of the 1840s, Barrett names this alternative model for the poet as the preacher, a comparison she never later undercuts or replaces. In 1843, she writes, "[I] do hold that the poet is a preacher," and, two years later, "poets...must preach their own doctrine...to be the means of any wisdom."[127]

If the role of the poet is similar to the role of the minister and the language of poetry is largely religious language, then poetry can have more purpose to the minister than just that of a tool in our hands. Poetry, as the voice of the poet, can minister to us in our own struggles, both personal and professional. In my own experience, poetry does all this and more. The four main ways that poetry ministers to me in my ministry, each deserving further exploration, are: naming the calling, expressing the divine, nurturing the spirit, and calling for justice.

Naming the Calling

One of the major messages of poetry is to call us into our deeper selves. This is the message of Webber's poem, and the message of so many others. As the poet Wendell Berry said:

The best art, I think, gives our highest impulses- reverence or love or com-passion or gratitude—an imagery or a language or a story that is necessary to them, to their effective life in this world…Art, I think, can help make life more full and abundant. It can help us survive as "living souls."[128]

One of the first poems to call me into my ministry was George Herbert's "The Collar," in which he struggles with the question of the priesthood, and the sacrifices it demands. In it, he argues against taking on the collar, the yoke of min-istry:

> What, shall I ever sigh and pine?
> My lines and life are free; free as the rode,
> Loose as the winde, as large as store.
> Shall I be still in suit?[129]

Suit here means the literal garments of priesthood, but also following the path, like following the suit in cards. Ultimately, the speaker in Herbert's poem, Herbert himself, does follow suit—the poem ends with God calling out to him and him responding.

Many, many other poems over the years have also put out this charge to heed our calling—this call to depth, to meaning, to vocation, to be true to humanity and our deepest selves. Mary Oliver issues the call in "The Summer Day" with those famous lines: "Tell me, what is it you plan to do / with your one wild and precious life?"[130] She says it again in "When Death Comes":

> When it's over, I want to say: all my life
> I was a bride married to amazement.
> I was the bridegroom, taking the world into my arms.
> When it's over, I don't want to wonder
> if I have made of my life something particular, and real.[131]

Likewise, in "Mindful" she says:

> It was what I was born for -
>   to look, to listen,
> to lose myself
>   inside this soft world -
>   to instruct myself
>   over and over.[132]

I have no doubt that Mary Oliver calls us to this awareness, to this depth of being, over and over and over again in her poetry. Rebecca Parker, president of Starr King School for the Ministry, calls us to it when she says, in "Choose to Bless the World":

> You must answer this question:
> What will you do with your gifts?
>
> *Choose to bless the world.*[133]

Lynn Ungar hears the call and calls us to it in "Camas Lilies":

> Even in sleep your life will shine.
> Make no mistake. Of course
> your work will always matter.[134]

Rainer Maria Rilke says it in "Archaic Torso of Apollo," simply, at the end: "You must change your life."[135] Rilke says it, too, in "Sonnets to Orpheus, Part Two, XII":

> Pour yourself like a fountain.
> Flow into the knowledge that what you are seeking
> Finishes often at the start, and, with ending begins.[136]

The poet William Stafford says it in "Ask Me":

> Some time when the river is ice ask me
> mistakes I have made. Ask me whether
> what I have done is my life.[137]

The Persian mystic poet Rumi said this many centuries ago, as well, in "A Community of the Spirit":

> There is a community of the spirit.
> Join it, and feel the delight
> of walking in the noisy street,
> and *being* the noise.[138]

What is the purpose of all this? The language of poetry is language that teaches us to look at things differently than the literal, mundane, usual way of looking at things, to see the world as an onion, or love as a rose, or faith as a mustard seed. Mary Oliver writes in "Lead":

I tell you this
to break your heart,
by which I mean only
that it break open and never close again
to the rest of the world. [139]

That's it, exactly. We are called by these poets to open our eyes to the rest of the world, to the spiritual and the physical, to the self and the other.

"What will you do with your one wild and precious life?" the poets ask, calling us to mindfulness, to attention, to being fully in the world and yet seeing beyond it. They instruct us to break open our hearts, join the community of the spirit, pour ourselves like a fountain, and "kill off all the top of one's head, remove it, and try to plunge deep into self, deep into memories, deep into the unconscious life." As Mary Oliver says, "Be ignited, or be gone"[140].

Expressing the Divine

Yeats wrote, "The purpose of rhythm, it has always seemed to me, is to prolong the moment of contemplation—the moment when we are both asleep and awake, which is the one moment of creation by hushing us with an alluring monotony, while it holds us waking by variety."[141] This spiritual function of poetry is perhaps the most obvious way in which the poet functions as minister. Sometimes it does it through its form, as Yeats suggests. Other times, it does it through its subject. Poetry gives voice to awe, to wonder, to beauty, to amazement. Mary Oliver, for example, makes this plain when she says she was a "bride married to amazement."[142] Oliver expresses awe and wonder and spirituality repeatedly in her writing, such as in "Circles" where she says:

I would like to live forever, but I am
content not to. Seeing what I have seen
has filled me; believing what I believe
has filled me.[143]

Many poets help us to understand awe and wonder through the beauty of language, or the poets may take a sight that very commonly can inspire awe and wonder—a mountain, the sky, the ocean—and crack it open and explain the awe, as Keats does in "On the Sea":

It keeps eternal whisperings around

Desolate shores, and with its mighty swell
Gluts twice ten thousand Caverns, till the spell
Of Hecate leaves them their old shadowy sound.[144]

Keats gives us the awe and beauty with a ministerial prescription to turn to it in our exhaustion, our turmoil, and see its vastness:

Oh ye! who have your eye-balls vexed and tired,
Feast them upon the wideness of the Sea...

Similarly, in the midst of a poem about justice, poet Sonia Sanchez offers us:

but we held out our eyes delirious with grace.
but we held out our eyes delirious with grace.[145]

She is telling us a secret: Grace helps us "stay on the battlefield" of life.

The poet Rumi names awe and wonder all the time, and sometimes draws us through that awe and wonder to something more, as in an untitled poem I have struggled with:

The grapes of my body can only become wine
after the winemaker tramples.
I surrender my spirit like grapes to his trampling
so my inmost heart can blaze and dance with joy.
Although the grapes go on weeping blood and sobbing
"I cannot bear any more anguish, any more cruelty,"
the trampler stuffs cotton in his ears: "I am not working in ignorance.
You can deny me if you want, you have every excuse,
but it is I who am the Master of this Work.
And when through my Passion you reach Perfection,
you will never be done praising my name."[146]

Lest we take ourselves too seriously, however, I turn briefly to Leonard Cohen, who writes of being expected to be a spiritual sage in "Leaving Mt. Baldy":

I finally understood
I had no gift
For Spiritual Matters...
A number of people
(some of them practitioners)
have begun to ask me angry questions
about The Ultimate Reality.

I suppose it's because
They don't like to see
old Jikan smoking.[147]

Oftentimes the poet will make us wake up to the holy with startling images that we would not think of as beautiful or awe-inspiring. Leonard Cohen, as a
minister to ministers, here reminds us of our humanity—that we don't have all the
answers about God and truth, about beauty and awe. We ministers are "old Jikan
smoking." Humorously, Leonard Cohen also writes a poem detailing the elaborate
Buddhist dressing ritual in "Early Morning at Mt. Baldy," including:

and finally the four-foot
serpentine belt
that twists into a huge handsome knot
resembling a braided *challah*.[148]

and ending with:

which I put on quickly
at 2:30 a.m.
over my enormous hard-on.[149]

On one level, it is purely humorous. Of course, it also says to the minister or
spiritual practitioner: You, too, are just another person, with your desires and your
failings, even as you put on the trappings of holiness. On another level, however, it
says that sexuality, too, is sacred, a tradition of embodied poetry that we see in Walt
Whitman, as well, as Greg Miller points out in "Spirituality and American Poetry":

Whitman claims, "I too had received identity by my body." For Whitman,
the daily and the bodily are holy. (How many poets write of armpits as giving
forth "divinest odors"?) He puts no stock in purity of religious identity, as he
writes in "Song of Myself": "Not objecting to special revelations, considering
a curl of smoke or a hair on the back of my hand just as curious as any revelation." For Whitman, the divine is in the temporal; flux itself is part of the
eternal, when experienced in its holiness.[150]

John Savant names this, as well:

Jacques Maritain tells us that "poetry is the saying of the ineffable." The
paradox here gets to the heart of the matter before us—and to the essential
nature of the poem. To put Maritain another way, poets use words to do what
words cannot do. What is "ineffable" refers to all those dimensions of experi-

ence that cannot be reduced to abstractions, that register their meanings or effects outside the context of predication or measurement, that are active in dream or memory or emotion or belief or artistic expression or intuition. Because they are thus irreducible, they participate to some degree in mystery.[151]

In that way, all things can participate to some degree in mystery, and the poet helps us see the sacredness in the ordinary, as well as in the majestic.

Sometimes the naming of the holy that poetry does is not through awe or wonder, or even embodiment; it can also be through moments of pain and the connection to the divine felt in those moments of piercing grief. Leonard Cohen writes in "The Beach at Kamini":

> All the world
> sudden and shining
> the moment before G-d
> turned you inward.[152]

Or consider the poetry of David Matias, a Unitarian Universalist about whom Greg Miller writes in "Spirituality and American Poetry":

> In his poems, David's voice, the voice in the process of defining itself, converses with voices and traditions of his own choosing. David's "Glimpses at a Destiny," beginning with a remembered epigraph from Ginsberg's "Kaddish," addresses God with the audacity of the Psalmist:
> Meanwhile his mother in Greece
> packs her suitcase, travels to America.
> Stay awake, God.
> She wants to see her son.[153]

The last loss of a relative in my own life was the loss of my grandfather—I got on a plane to Georgia to go see him in the hospital, only to find him dead when I arrived. This poem speaks of that kind of agonizing hope while traveling to see a dying loved one simply and eloquently: "Stay awake, God."

Nurturing the Spirit

If poetry begins a ministry by calling us into our deepest selves and expressing the divine, it continues this ministry in an inward focus by calling us to come into contact with woundedness in ourselves and others. Poetry first teaches us to minister to ourselves in our pain and sorrow through calling us to turn inward to our deepest selves, requiring coming into contact with the deepest wounds. Poetry does three things with sorrow. It gives voice to the sorrow; it helps heal the sorrow, and it tells us how to use the sorrow.

Giving Voice to Sorrow: We all know that in times of grief, we often turn to our religion. Likewise, in times of grief we also turn toward poetry. Furthermore, in times of ministering to grief, ministers turn to poetry, as well, for the language to express sorrow. If you walk into any funeral parlor, you will find the poem "Footprints" available somewhere on a card, bookmark, poster or pamphlet. That's the one that ends: "The Lord replied, 'The years when you have seen only one set of footprints, my child, is when I carried you.'"[154] Any minister who has been around for any length of time has been asked to read that poem during at least one funeral. I don't care for it personally—it is not my theology—but I can see how it seems to comfort a lot of people in times of grief. It is performing a ministry, humble servant though it is.

I will never forget a moment I had where poetry broke open someone to the fountain of grief. I had turned to W.H. Auden's poem "Funeral Blues" when thinking of the death of a relative of a congregant. When I shared it with that member, it brought forth a fountain of tears—tears that had been held back, and tears that I hope were healing ones. The poem is used in the film *Four Weddings and a Funeral*, which is what brought it to mind. Its last two stanzas read:

> He was my North, my South, my East and West,
> My working week and my Sunday rest,
> My noon, my midnight, my talk, my song;
> I thought that love would last forever: I was wrong.
> The stars are not wanted now; put out every one,
> Pack up the moon and dismantle the sun,
> Pour away the ocean and sweep up the woods;
> For nothing now can ever come to any good.[155]

The grief Auden expresses is the raw grief in the newness of death. In my own experience with this poem, Auden gave voice to grief through the language of poetry that was not possible for someone experiencing that raw grief himself. The poem became the voice of ministry in our time together.

Grief is expressed so well by Donald Hall in his book *Without*, a series of poems written during his wife's battle with leukemia and during the year after her death. The poem right at her death, "Without," captures the pain more eloquently than would be possible in prose. He writes:

we lived in a small island stone nation
without color under gray clouds and wind
distant the unlimited ocean acute
lymphoblastic leukemia without seagulls
or palm trees without vegetation
or animal life only barnacles and lead
colored moss that darkened when months did.
hours days weeks months weeks days hours
the year endured without punctuation
february without ice winter sleet
snow melted recovered but nothing
without thaw although cold streams hurtled
no snowdrop or crocus rose no yellow
no red leaves of maple without October.[156]

Part of what makes you feel his intolerable pain as you read is the repetition: no, no, no, without, without, without. The lack of capitalization and commas or other punctuation makes each line flow endlessly into the next. In the lack of all these things—no seasons, no punctuation—you see the unendingness of gray life without her.

We turn to poetry in grief, and we turn to scripture—not always because we believe in scripture, but because that scripture is poetry. For example, the lines, "Yea, though I walk through the valley of the shadow of death," are always more eloquent in the more poetic, formalized language of the King James Bible. They are more able to get at the mystery beyond grief through the use of poetic language than it would be with any other translation. We turn to the poetry for comfort, as Spencer Reece explains through his experience of being a Hospice Chaplain: "Christians, Muslims, Jews, Buddhists, agnostics enter Hospice. We, the nondenominational volunteers, sometimes proselytize, but more often than not hold a hand, read a chapter from the Bible or the Koran, or even, sometimes, a poem."[157] The poetry Reece turns to in order to sustain him is the poetry of George Herbert, such as the poem "Sacrifice," about which Reece says:

> If poems are elemental, then Herbert's are made of air, barely anchored by dirt and water. Neither do they blaze with the fires of rancor and frustration as John Donne's battering of the heart does. This begins with "The Sacrifice," where the plangent refrain, "Was ever grief like mine?" repeats like the dripping of Christ's blood on the cross. Each of his poems is influenced by the reality of Christ on the cross.[158]

Reece's theology is not mine, but I can see that Herbert's naming of Jesus' suffering with the refrain "Was ever grief like mine?" is a naming of all suffering, inviting people to think of their own suffering, even while naming Jesus' as greater.

A poem for me which dramatically names the suffering of a people is the Holocaust poem "The Butterfly" written by Pavel Friedman, who died at age 23 in Auschwitz. He wrote of the sorrow of the ghetto, saying:

> The dandelions call to me
> And the white chestnut branches in the court.
> Only I never saw another butterfly
> That butterfly was the last one.
> Butterflies don't live in here, in the ghetto.[159]

Poems such as these name the grief we carry. As said in, "For the Sake of Strangers," by Dorianne Laux:

> No matter what the grief, its weight,
> we are obliged to carry it.
> We rise and gather momentum, the dull strength,
> that pushes us through crowds.[160]

We push ourselves onward from our grief, continuing to live our lives in the world.

Healing from the Sorrow: Sometimes the act of writing poetry alone can be a balm to the soul. Karen Sprow writes in an article titled, "Spirituality with Poetic Assistance":

> Writing poetry has helped me find some clarity in my spiritual beliefs. Poetry is a way to express our emotions and feelings, clearing them out of the way for the essence, or soul, to float to the front of our thoughts. Poetry has also allowed me to question my beliefs and values, which leads to searching for answers. My poetry is filled with questions, probably more questions than statements. But just in forming a question, one must explore what exactly must be questioned and what the possible answers might be.[161]

Other times, the poem, through telling us the process of the grief cycle, helps us along it. For example, consider the poem "The Gardener" by Robin Becker, which talks first about the stage of denial, saying:

> She works and works against sadness
> stilling grief with a spade
> Only the dead have come

home to their faithful hungers
and in the spring, when they speak, she opens
the ground and puts in something
green the dead can climb. Small pine
and spruce in their poor burlap.
Lilacs. Dogwood.[162]

It is significant that she invokes dogwood at the end of the stanza, in a sentence all by itself: Dogwood, period. Dogwood is a tree that itself symbolizes a type of grief—grief in the tree that has been used as a symbol of the crucifixion, as shown in the anonymous poem called "The Dogwood Tree":

All who see it will think of Me,
Nailed to a cross from a dogwood tree.
Protected and cherished this tree shall be
A reflection to all of My agony.[163]

Contemporary Arab poet Saniyya Saleh writes about another coping mechanism for grief in her poem, "Exile," in which she writes:

For grief
he wore those colorful bells,
a mask of joy.
He bound his stories
to his tongue's tip
so they would not betray him
at the crucial moment.[164]

Sometimes the healing from grief in poetry comes not from learning about the grief cycle, but from the poem teaching us to look beyond our own pain, to the ultimate, or to the universe. Hayden Carruth in his poem, "Ecstasy," calls ecstasy, "the great pain assuaged,"[165] about which Roger Housden writes:

Surely it is this, even without knowing it, that we all long for deep in our bones: *ekstasis*, the experience of being lifted out of our bodies, our pains, our sadness, and our cares, then set down, at least for a lifetime, in a life where we are one with the current of all life, where we know that all is already well, and shall always be well.[166]

The mystic Christian Julian of Norwich wrote "All will be well," a phrase Unitarian Universalist minister Meg Barnhouse turned into a song exploring her struggle with the phrase. Theology, music, and poetry give us this confusing, seemingly paradoxical message that all will be well. It is not meant to lightly brush away sadness and pain, but that there is a time when we will be one with the current of all life—and that is *well*. Similarly, in the poem "Sunset," Rainer Maria Rilke says:

> You look, and soon these two world both leave you,
> one part climbs toward heaven, one sinks to earth…
> leaving you (it is impossible to untangle the threads)
> your own life, timid and standing high and growing,
> so that, sometimes blocked in, sometimes reaching out,
> one moment your life is a stone in you, and the next, a star.[167]

Poetry shows us that the stone lifts from our hearts, that grief can end, that "all will be well."

Using the Sorrow: Understanding our own pain and suffering, our own sorrows, is a key to being able to minister in the world. Mary Oliver writes of this in "The Uses of Sorrow":

> Someone I loved once gave me
> a box full of darkness.
> It took me years to understand
> that this, too, was a gift.[168]

In a more traditional Christian faith, one might link one's own sorrow with the suffering of Jesus, and use one's own pain to better understand one's faith. In our faith, I think we're more likely to see the use of understanding our own pain as a key to understanding others. We all can tell stories about how some hardship we endured taught us something we needed to learn. Sometimes it is perseverance, or inner strength. One of the major lessons of hardship is learning compassion and empathy. As the poet Naomi Shihab Nye writes:

> Before you know what kindness really is
> you must lose things,
> feel the future dissolve in a moment
> like salt in a weakened broth.
> What you held in your hand,
> what you counted and carefully saved,
> all this must go so you know
> how desolate the landscape can be
> between the regions of kindness.[169]

Once we have turned our grief into a strength from which we find empathy; we begin to be able to do what the poet Hafiz urges us to do in the poem, "With That Moon Language," in order to live out that compassion:

Everyone you see, you say to them, "Love me."
Of course you do not do this out loud; otherwise,
someone would call the cops.
Still, though, think about this, this great pull in us
to connect.
Why not become the one who lives with a full moon
in each eye that is always saying,
with that sweet moon language,
what every other eye in this world is dying to hear?[170]

Hafiz is calling us, again, the poet calling us to live our deepest selves and, this time, more: to respond to the deepest wounds of the world, a calling which leads us to justice.

Calling for Justice

The healing nature of poetry and the social justice calling of poetry are not unrelated. Poet and physician Peter Pereira writes, after talking about poetry as a healing power:

Finally, I think the reading and writing of poems is also a way to heal the world…Carolyn Forch, a former Amnesty International worker and poet who edited a wonderful anthology, Against Forgetting: Twentieth-Century Poetry of Witness, said:
"One of the things that happens when poets bear witness to historical events is that everyone they tell becomes a witness, too; everyone they tell also becomes responsible for what they have heard and what they now know."
Poetry of witness has long been a way that cultures and civilizations all over the world remember things—their war stories, their cultural milestones— and give voice to the oppressed or the disappeared.[171]

Poet Adrienne Rich says, "I see poetry in the United States as coming out of the points of stress in our society."[172] There are moments in society where the role of the poet is crystal clear, and we stand up and take notice of the way their shining words cut through the pretenses of the world and lay bare the truth for all to see. What they are doing is calling us, through poetry, to the work of social justice.

A recurring moment in our culture when we suddenly take notice of poets calling us to this work is when we hear an inaugural poem at the inauguration of a new president. The two inaugural poems which stand out to me as calls to justice are Maya Angelou's at the inauguration of Bill Clinton, and Elizabeth Alexander's at the inauguration of Barack Obama. A snippet from Angelou's poem, "On the Pulse of Morning," says:

> Lift up your faces, you have a piercing need
> For this bright morning dawning for you.
> History, despite its wrenching pain,
> Cannot be unlived, and if faced with courage,
> Need not be lived again.
> Lift up your eyes upon
> The day breaking for you.
> Give birth again
> To the dream.
> Women, children, men,
> Take it into the palms of your hands.[173]

Angelou's words give us the yearning for social justice in our country, along with the view of our country not as becoming greater through westward expansion, but through increasingly becoming a place of freedom and equality. It calls to my mind another famous poem that has a permanent spot in our nation: on the Statue of Liberty. Almost, but not yet, trite with age, the words of Emma Lazarus' poem "The New Colossus" still have the power to move me each time I read them:

> "Keep ancient lands, your storied pomp!" cries she
> With silent lips. "Give me your tired, your poor,
> Your huddled masses yearning to breathe free,
> The wretched refuse of your teeming shore.
> Send these, the homeless, tempest-tost to me.[174]

Then, more recently, we were given a new inaugural poem by Elizabeth Alexander, "Praise Song for the Day," in which she says:

> What if the mightiest word is love?
> Love beyond marital, filial, national,
> love that casts a widening pool of light,
> love with no need to pre-empt grievance.
> In today's sharp sparkle, this winter air,

any thing can be made, any sentence begun.
On the brink, on the brim, on the cusp.[175]

As a piece of our national discourse, these words held an important place in an important moment, where we did feel "on the brink, on the brim, on the cusp," waiting to see if we would fulfill the dreams for our country's future where the greatest of these is love, the dream set forth by Emma Lazarus.

In ministry, we say that one of our jobs is to "speak the truth to power." That means speaking up for the truth, even when speaking the truth puts us at risk because it is not what those in power wish to hear. We must speak truth to power. When Bill Moyers asked, "What does poetry have to say to power?" of poet Rita Dove, he showed that this role we have as ministers is also a role that poets have, to speak truth to power. Rita Dove answers:

> By making us stop for a moment, poetry gives us an opportunity to think about ourselves as human beings on this planet and what we mean to each other. In that way, poetry becomes a voice to power that says, "Power is not the end-all or the be-all." Equally important is the connection poetry emphasizes of human being to human being: what *are* we doing to make the lives of everyone better, and not just materially but spiritually as well? I think that's why poetry has often been considered dangerous.[176]

These poems illustrate a way in which poetry moves into our national discourse and operates from a place of authority; however, poetry can also be countercultural—a voice crying, like the prophets, against what the kingdom has become. Both of these types of poetry call us to a type of ministry, a type of social justice, of living our values in the world.

Some of the most powerful examples of poetry that calls us to justice are poems in our country that call us to civil rights. Of course, in this tradition of poetry that expresses the struggles of a people, we place the powerful poetry of Langston Hughes. In "Let America Be America Again," he says:

> O, let my land be a land where Liberty
> Is crowned with no false patriotic wreath,
> But opportunity is real, and life is free,
> Equality is in the air we breathe.
> (There's never been equality for me,
> Nor freedom in this "homeland of the free.")[177]

Hughes ends:

We, the people, must redeem
The land, the mines, the plants, the rivers.
The mountains and the endless plain—
All, all the stretch of these great green states—
And make America again![178]

Similarly powerful is the poetry of James Weldon Johnson, who wrote the poem "Lift Every Voice and Sing," that became the hymn known as the black national anthem, and who wrote in "Fifty Years," for the fiftieth anniversary of the signing of the "Emancipation Proclamation," fifty years before Martin Luther King, Jr. would stand there and say, "I have a dream":

That for which millions prayed and sighed,
That for which tens of thousands fought,
For which so many freely died,
God cannot let it come to naught.[179]

We all know that the music of the civil rights movement was an important tool in shaping our country's destiny through the non-violent struggle for civil rights and human equality. We also know that poetry is the basis for song, but we can easily overlook it, and overlook the poetry that wasn't song that helped change our nation. A lot of poetry about justice names the injustice, drawing the picture of it in poignant terms, informing us, drawing us into the lives of the other.

Indeed, a lot of poetry names the injustice, but some goes even further, and calls us into action, demanding of us that we, too, become the prophet poet and speak out against it, as it does. Sonia Sanchez wrote a poem for the group Sweet Honey in the Rock which says:

i say come, wrap your feet around justice
i say come, wrap your tongues around truth
i say come, wrap your hands with deeds and prayer.[180]

Prophetic poetic words that call me to justice are ones such as the ones by Rebecca Parker that I've quoted so often: "Choose to bless the world." The words of poet prophet Pablo Neruda in "So Is My Life" similarly call for a view wherein each person is responsible for blessing the world:

My duty moves along with my song:
I am I am not: that is my destiny.
I exist not if I do not attend to the pain
of those who suffer: they are my pains.

For I cannot be without existing for all,
for all who are silent and oppressed. [181]

The hard part about the justice work that our faith calls us to is that it is endless. It is easy to despair, when so much is left to do at the end of the day, and nothing is ever completely resolved. When I reach that point where I need ministering to, when I need to be reminded of why we do what we do and that this is our sacred and religious obligation, I turn to words from "Natural Resources," by Adrienne Rich, the same ones I turned to after the Twin Towers fell, words that are in the hymnal *Singing the Living Tradition*. She writes:

My heart is moved by all I cannot save:
So much has been destroyed
I have to cast my lot with those who, age after age,
perversely, with no extraordinary power, reconstitute the world.[182]

This is our job as ministers; this is what poetry calls us to; this is our ministry as Unitarian Universalists in this world; this is how we speak the truth to power: We cast our lots with those who, age after age, perversely, with no extraordinary power, reconstitute the world.

Conclusion

Poetry calls us into our deepest selves; gives voice to the awe and wonder and the sense of the divine; opens up, names, and heals the woundedness of our spirits; and calls us into justice work for the world. There are many more ways in which poetry functions as ministry in our lives and poets function as ministers and vice versa. As religious leaders, as ministers, we can turn to poetry for a source of inspiration, a source of comfort, or to give us the fire of commitment. Without needing to analyze rhyme and meter, without understanding alliteration or assonance, or the difference between elegy and epigram, we can understand how the words "to break your heart, / by which I mean only / that it break open and never close again / to the rest of the world" are words of ministry, calling us into ministry, expressing the divine, teaching us about healing, and calling us into justice.

Endnotes

1   Andrew C. Kennedy, "Silent Retreats," Everyday Spiritual Practice. Ed. Scott W. Alexander. (Boston: Skinner House Books, 2001), 41-46.

2   Ibid.

3   Ibid.

4   Jesus Seminar on the Road, Jackson, MI October 2010.

5   Sophia Lyon Fahs, "It Matters What We Believe," Singing the Living Tradition. (Boston: Beacon Press, 1993).

6   Information from <http://www.godhatesfags.com>.

7   Again, with thanks to Andrew C. Kennedy. For more, see Andrew C. Kennedy, "Silent Retreats," Everyday Spiritual Practice. Ed. Scott W. Alexander. (Boston: Skinner House Books, 2001), 41-46.

8   Peter Morales, "A Larger Love: A Valentine's Day Message from the President of the UUA." (Boston: Unitarian Universalist Association, 13 February 2010), <http://www.uua.org/news/newssubmissions/158319.shtml>.

9   Cecilia Kingman, "This Minister Is Standing on the Side of Love," The Wenatchee World (Wenatchee, 12 February 2010) <http://www.wenatcheeworld.com/news/2010/feb/12/this-minister-is-standing-on-the-side-of-love/>

10   Sarah Hagan, "Standing on the Side of Love at SUNY Potsdam" (Time Warner, 13 February 2010) <http://news10now.com/watertown-north-news-1052-content/top_stories/496054/standing-on-the-side-of-love-at-suny-potsdam>.

11   "Maryland Pastor to Stop Signing Marriage Certificates" D.C. Agenda (February 2010) <http://dcagenda.com/2010/02/md-pastor-to-stop-signing-marriage-certificates/>

12   Theresa Novak, Letter, Standing on the Side of Love (30 January 2010) <http://www.standingonthesideoflove.org/2010/01/>

13   Sean Dennison, "Speaking on Behalf of Love," Ministrare <http://revsean.wordpress.com/category/standing-on-the-side-of-love/>.

14   Meg Riley, "Minnesota Kicks-Off Reimagining Valentine's Day," Standing on the Side of Love, 10 February 2010, <http://www.standingonthesideoflove.org/blog/minnesotas-kicks-off-reimagining-valentines-day/>

15   Peter Morales, "A Larger Love: A Valentine's Day Message from the President of the UUA (Boston: Unitarian Universalist Association, 13 February, 2010) <http://www.uua.org/news/newssubmissions/158319.shtml> .

16   William Sinkford, "Rev. William G. Sinkford's Remarks from Service of Healing Following Knoxville, Tennessee, Tragedy" July 29, 2008. <http://www.uua.org/news/newssubmissions/117463.shtml>.

17   David R. Shaffer, Social and Personality Development, Sixth Ed., 333.

18   Richard S. Gilbert, Building Your Own Theology, 71.

19   Vicktor Frankel, Man's Search for Meaning, 90.

20   Richard S. Gilbert, Building Your Own Theology, 70.

21   Parker Palmer, Let Your Life Speak: Listening for the Voice of Vocation (New York: Jossey-Bass, 1999), 3.

22   Parker Palmer, 11.

23   Margaret Silf, One Hundred Wisdom Stories from around the World (Cleveland, OH: Pilgrim, 2003), 157-158.

24   Kurt Vonnegut, Jr., Fates Worse than Death, qtd. at <http://atheism.about.com/library/quotes/bl_q_KVonnegut.htm>.

25   "News In the Congregations," UU World (Boston: Unitarian Universalist Association, 2002), <http://www.uuworld.org/2004/02/newsinthecongregations.html>

26   Kurt Vonnegut, Jr., Palm Sunday, 198-199.

27   Tim Jensen, "Death...and Taxes...." <http://www.uucarlisle.org/sermons/20062007/apr1507.htm>

28   Kurt Vonnegut, Jr., "Yes, We Have No Nirvanas,"Wampeters, Foma & Grandfalloons, 31.

29   Dan Wakefield, "Open-Hearted in Fiction and Friendship," April 29, 2007, The Boston Globe. <http://www.boston.com/ae/books/articles/2007/04/29/open_hearted_in_fiction_and_friendship/?page=full>

30   Kurt Vonnegut, Jr., Palm Sunday, 175.

31   Kurt Vonnegut Jr., quoted in 2000 Years of Disbelief, Famous People with the Courage to Doubt, by James A. Haught, Prometheus Books, 1996. <http://atheism.about.com/library/quotes/bl_q_KVonnegut.htm>

32   Kurt Vonnegut, Jr., God Bless You, Dr. Kevorkian, 45.

33   Kurt Vonnegut, Jr., God Bless You, Dr. Kevorkian, 77.

34   Kurt Vonnegut, Jr, Slaughterhouse-Five, 22.

35   Kurt Vonnegut, Jr., Palm Sunday, 84.

36   Kurt Vonnegut, Jr. Wikepedia. <http://en.wikipedia.org/wiki/Kurt_Vonnegut>

37   Kurt Vonnegut, Jr., Palm Sunday, 5.

38   Kurt Vonnegut, Jr., Palm Sunday, 194.

39   Norman Perrin, "Rediscovering the Teachings of Jesus by Norman Perrin,"<http://www.religion-online.org/showchapter.asp?title=1564&C=1449>.

40   James W. Fowler, Stages of Faith: The Psychology of Human Development and the Quest for Meaning (New York: HarperSanFrancisco, 1981).

41   James W. Fowler, Stages of Faith: The Psychology of Human Development and the Quest for Meaning (New York: HarperSanFrancisco, 1981), 173.

42   Robert W. Funk, Roy W. Hoover, and the Jesus Seminar, The Five Gospels: The Search for the Authentic Words of Jesus (New York: HarperSanFrancisco, 1993), 75.

43   Marcus Borg, Meeting Jesus Again for the First Time: The Historical Jesus & the Heart of Contemporary Faith (San Francisco: Harper Collins, 1994), 24.

44   Susannah Wilder Heinz, "Who Do Men Say That I Am?" A Study of Jesus (Boston: Beacon Press, 1965), 44.

45   Ibid, 46-7.

46   Ibid, 49.

47   Ibid, 51.

48   Ibid, 30.

49   Robert W. Funk, Roy W. Hoover, and the Jesus Seminar, 6.

50   John Dominic Crossan, Who Killed Jesus: Exposing the Roots of Anti-Semitism in the Gospel Story of the Death of Jesus (New York: HarperSanFrancisco, 1995), 1.

51   Stephen Prothero, American Jesus: How the Son of God Became a National Icon (New York: Farrar, Straus and Giroux, 2003), 230.

52   Anonymous, "UUA Forums: Jesus: Was He God?" (Posted: Nov 18, 2005 23:46:08). Available at <http://www.uua.org/programs/forums/ index.php?action=vthread&forum=3&topic=245>.

53   Anonymous, "UUA Forums: Jesus—Neither Literal Son of God nor God" (Posted: Apr 4, 2006 23:22:37). Available from <http://www.uua.org/programs/forums/ index.php?action=vthread&forum=3&topic=294>.

54   William L. Landrum, letter to author, November 10, 2006.

55   Michael Baigent, Richard Leigh, and Henry Lincoln, Holy Blood, Holy Grail (New York: Dell Publishing, 1982), 354.

56   Susan Smith, "The Truth About Santa," UU World 20, no. 4 (2006): 24-25.

57   F. Forrester Church, Preface, The Jefferson Bible, Thomas Jefferson (Boston: Beacon Press, 1989), viii.

58   Sophia Lyon Fahs, Jesus the Carpenter's Son (Boston: Beacon Press, 1945), 159.

59   Bruce Southworth, ed., "UU Views of Jesus" (Boston: Unitarian Universalist Association, 2006). Available from <http://www.uua.org/pamphlet/3040.html>.

60   Caroline W. Landrum, letter to author, 6 November 6, 2007.

61   Prescott B. Wintersteen, Christology in American Unitarianism: An Anthology of Nineteenth and Twentieth Century Unitarian Theologians (Boston: Unitarian Universalist Christian Fellowship, 1977), 137.

62   Ibid, 138-139.

63   Erik Reece, "Jesus Without the Miracles: Thomas Jefferson's Bible and the Gospel of Thomas," Harper's Magazine 311, no.1867, December 2005.

64   Elaine Pagels, Beyond Belief: The Secret Gospel of Thomas (New York: Vintage Books, 2003), 229.

65   Ibid, 229.

66   Alice Blair Wesley, "Our Unitarian Universalist Faith: Frequently Asked Questions" (Boston: Unitarian Universalist Association, 2006). <http://www.uua.org/aboutuu/uufaq.html>.

67   Bruce Southworth, Editor, "UU Views of Jesus" (Boston: UUA Press, 1985). Pamphlet.

68   Ibid.

69   Susannah Wilder Heinz, 14-15.

70   The American Heritage Dictionary, The Second College Ed., (Boston: Houghton Mifflin Company, 1985), s.v. "prophet."

71   Bruce Chilton, Rabbi Jesus: An Intimate Biography (New York: Doubleday, 2000), 13.

72   Stephen Prothero, 214.

73   Bruce Chilton, 39.

74   Marcus Borg, 54.

75   Ibid, 59.

76   Robert W. Funk, Roy W. Hoover, and the Jesus Seminar, 5.

77   Elaine Pagels, 229.

78   "2 Definitions and Differences." (Nashua, NH: Unitarian Universalist Church of Nashua, NH: 1994-2000). Available at <http://www.uunashua.org/100q/c2.shtml>.

79   Jennifer Owens-O'Quill, "Alive Again: Jesus and the Legacy of the Resurrection" (Chicago, Second Unitarian Church: April 11, 2004). <http://home.att.net/~secondunitarian/sermon_4_11_2004.html>.

80   Robert W. Funk, Honest to Jesus: Jesus for a New Millennium (New York: HarperSanFrancisco, 1996), 152-158.

81   Robert W. Funk, Roy W. Hoover, and the Jesus Seminar, 75.

82   Susannah Wilder Heinz, 14.

83   Alice Blair Wesley, "Our Unitarian Universalist Faith: Frequently Asked Questions."

84   Bruce Southworth, Editor, "UU Views of Jesus" (Boston: UUA Press, 1985). Pamphlet.

85   Elaine Pagels, 229.

86   Marcus Borg, 13-20.

87   Ibid, 9.

88   Robert W. Funk, Roy W. Hoover, and the Jesus Seminar, 6.

89   Ibid, 6.

90   James W. Fowler, 198.

91   Ibid, 200.

92   David Bumbaugh, Unitarian Universalism: A Narrative History (Chicago: Meadville Lombard Press, 2000), 46-47.

93   Charles A. Howe, For Faith and Freedom (Boston: Skinner House Books, 1997), 143.

94   Daniel Jonah Goldhagen, Hitler's Willing Executioners: Ordinary Germans and the Holocaust (New York: Vintage, 1997), 417.

95   Philip Zimbardo, "For Goodness' Sake," O Magazine (April 2007), 199-202.

96   Zeno Franco and Philip Zimbardo, "The Banality of Evil," Greater Good Magazine (Fall/Winter 2006-2007), <http://www.november.org/BottomsUp/reading/banality.html>.

97   Administrator, "Art of Mindful Living—Solitude," Plum Village (15 August 2009) <http://www.plumvillage.org/practice.html?start=20>.

98   Introduction, "A Class Divided," Frontline (PBS), <http://www.pbs.org/wgbh/pages/frontline/shows/divided/etc/synopsis.html>.

99   Po Bronson and Ashley Merryman, NurtureShock (New York: Hachette Book Group, 2009), 49.

100 Ibid., 50-51.

101 Ibid., 66.

102 Ibid., 52-3.

103 Ibid., 53.

104 Michael Hlinka, "There must be a direct connection between CEO pay, performance." CBC News. February 5, 2009. <http://www.cbc.ca/money/moneytalks/2009/02/michael_hlinka_there_must_be_a.html>

105 Barack Obama, "Should Security Guards Wear Bullet-Proof Vests?; President Obama Urges Health Care Changes." CNN. June 11, 2009 <http://transcripts.cnn.com/TRANSCRIPTS/0906/11/cnr.05.html>.

106 James Ledbetter, "Give Us Your Tired, Your Poor. Really. We Mean It," Slate, 2 September 2010, <http://www.slate.com/id/2265974/>.

107   Jennifer Ludden, "Barriers Abound for Immigrants Learning English," (National Public Radio, 2007), <http://www.npr.org/templates/story/story.php?storyId=14330106>.

108   "The Economics of (Im)migration," (Boston: Unitarian Universalist Association), <http://www.uua.org/documents/washingtonoffice/immigration/study-guides/iic.pdf>.

109   Elie Wiesel, qtd in Writing: A Guide to College and Beyond. Brief Second Edition. Ed. Lester Faigley. New York: Longman, 2010. 500.

110   Ivan Nikolav, 08 August 2010. <http://www.citizenorange.com/orange/2010/08/dream-now-letters-to-barack-ob.html>

111   Jose Franco, "Jose Franco on the Dream Act," YouTube, <http://www.youtube.com/watch?v=cL4s9hruQqc>.

112   John Steinbeck, The Grapes of Wrath, John Steinbeck Centennial Edition (New York: Penguin Books, 2002) 32.

113   Ibid., 349.

114   Ibid., 95.

115   Ibid., 434-435.

116   Ibid., 423.

117   Ibid., 418.

118   Ibid., 419.

119   James Poniewozik, "CNBC Under Fire: Sticking Up for the Big Guy?" Time Magazine (12 Mar. 2009) Web. 26 Mar. 2011. <http://www.time.com/time/arts/article/0,8599,1884328,00.html>.

120   Laurel Hallman, "Images for Our Lives," Lecture, The Ministerial Conference at Berry Street (Boston. 26 June 2003), Unitarian Universalist Ministers Association: Wed. 7 Aug. 2009, <http://www.uuma.org/BerryStreet/Essays/BSE2003.htm>.

121   Bill Moyers, The Language of Life (New York: Main Street Books, 1996), 112.

122   Colleen Morton Busch, "Poetry Flesh, Zen Bones." Tricycle. 15.3 (Spring 2006): 72-5.

123   Garrison Keillor, Good Poems for Hard Times (New York: Penguin, 2006), xvii.

124   Bill Moyers, xvi.

125   Ibid., xiv.

126   Christine Lore Webber, "Mother Wisdom Speaks," Womanprayers: Prayers by Women throughout History and Around the World. Mary Ford-Grabowsky, Ed. (San Francisco: HarperSanFrancisco, 2003), 123-24. Qtd. in <http://seekingauthenticvoice.blogspot.com/2009/06/mother-wisdom-speaks.html>.

127 Karen Dieleman, "Elizabeth Barrett Browning's Religious Poetics: Congregationalist Models of Hymnist and Preacher," Victorian Poetry. (45.2: Summer 2007), 136.

128 Harold K. Bush, "Wendell Berry, Seeds of Hope, and the Survival of Creation," Christianity & Literature (56.2: Winter 2007), 297-316, WilsonSelect, Wed. 22 July 2009, 300.

129 George Herbert, "The Collar," The Norton Anthology of English Literature, Fifth ed. (New York: W.W. Norton & Company, 1986), 1349-350, 1349.

130 Mary Oliver, New and Selected Poems, Volume I (Boston: Beacon, 1992).

131 Mary Oliver, "When Death Comes," Ten poems to Last a Lifetime by Roger Housden (New York: Harmony Books, 2004), 111. Print.

132 Mary Oliver, New, Vol. 1 90-91.

133 Rebecca Parker, "Choose to Bless the World," Qtd. in "A Description of Our Religious Community," <http://www.fusf.org/community/index.html>, 16 Oct. 2009.

134 Lynn Ungar, Blessing the Bread, (Boston: Skinner House Books, 1995).

135 Rainer Maria Rilke, "Archaic Torso of Apollo," Qtd. in Poets.Org, <http://www.poets.org/viewmedia.php/prmMID/15814>, 16 Oct. 2009.

136 Rainer Maria Rilke, "Sonnets to Orpheus, Part Two, XII," Ten Poems to Change Your Life Again and Again, By Housden, Roger (New York: Harmony, 2007), 21-22, 21.

137 William Stafford, "Ask Me," PoemHunter.Com, <http://www.poemhunter.com/poem/ask-me/>, 16 Oct. 2009.

138 Jalāl ad-Dīn Muhammad Rumi, "A Community of the Spirit," Reading, In the Arms of the Beloved: The Poetry of Rumi, Church of the Larger Fellowship (Boston, 14 Oct. 2009), <http://clf.uua.org>.

139 Mary Oliver, New and Selected Poems, Volume II (Boston: Beacon, 2005), 54.

140 Mary Oliver, New, Vol. 2 57.

141 D. Graham Burnett, "'Joy in Repetition': Poetry, Prayer, and the Purpose of Rhythm," The American Poetry Review (37.4: July/August 2008), 11-13, WilsonSelect, Wed. 22 July 2009, 12

142 Mary Oliver, "When" 111.

143 Mary Oliver, New, Vol. 2 30.

144 John Keats, "On the Sea," The Norton Anthology of English Literature, Fifth ed. (New York: W.W. Norton & Company, 1986), 801.

145 Sonia Sanchez, Shake Loose My Skin New and Selected Poems (Bluestreak) (New York: Beacon, 2000), 149.

146   Jatil ad-Dīn Muhammad Rumi, "Untitled," Reading, In the Arms of the Beloved: The Poetry of Rumi, Church of the Larger Fellowship (Boston, 14 Oct. 2009), <http://clf.uua.org>.

147   Leonard Cohen, Book of Longing (New York: Ecco, 2006), 22.

148   Ibid., 21.

149   Ibid., 21.

150   Greg Miller, "Spirituality and American Poetry," Tikkun (18.1: 2003): 68-70, WilsonSelect, 07 Oct. 2009.

151   John Savant, "Of sacrament and poetry," America, (180.9: March 20 1999): 12-14+, WilsonSelect, Wed. 22 July 2009.

152   Leonard Cohen, Book of Longing (New York: Ecco, 2006), 80.

153   Miller.

154   Mary Stevenson, "Footprints in the Sand," "Footprints in the Sand: An Amazing Poem in Search of Its Author," Wowzone.Com, <http://www.wowzone.com/fprints.htm>, 17 Oct. 2009.

155   W.H. Auden, "Funeral Blues," PoemHunter.Com, 16 Oct. 2009, <http://www.poemhunter.com/poem/funeral-blues-2/>.

156   Donald Hall, Without (Boston: Houghton Mifflin Company, 1998), 46.

157   Spencer Reece, "Two Hospice Essays," The American Poetry Review, (37.2: March/April 2008): 31-4, WilsonSelect, Wed. 22 July 2009, 32

158   Ibid 34.

159   Pavel Friedman, "I Never Saw Another Butterfly," Shoah Education Project Web, <http://www.shoaheducation.com/butterfly.html>, 17 Oct. 2009.

160   Dorianne Laux, "For the Sake of Strangers," Ten Poems to Change Your Life Again and Again, By Housden, Roger (New York: Harmony, 2007), 57

161   Karin Sprow, "Spirituality with Poetic Assistance," Adult Learning, (17.1-4: 2006): 7-10, WilsonSelect, Wed. 22 July 2009, 9.

162   Marilyn Sewell, Cries of The Spirit (New York: Beacon, 2000), 161-162.

163   Anonymous, "The Dogwood Tree," Ellen Bailey Poems, 17 Oct. 2009, <http://www.ellenbailey.com/poems/ellen_140.htm>.

164   Nathalie Handal, Ed, The Poetry of Arab Women: A Contemporary Anthology (New York: Interlink Books, 2001), 268.

165   Roger Housden, Ten poems to Last a Lifetime (New York: Harmony Books, 2004), 30.

166   Ibid., 31.

167   Ibid., 49.

168   Mary Oliver, Thirst (Boston: Beacon Press, 2006), 52.

169   Naomi Shihab Nye, "Kindness," Panhala, 17 Oct. 2009, <http://www.panhala.net/Archive/Kindness.html>.

170   Roger Housden, Ten Poems to Change Your Life Again and Again (New York: Harmony, 2007), 107.

171   Peter Pereira, "The Healing Power of Poetry," The Writer (120.3: 2007): 15-17, Wilson Select, 07 Oct. 2009.

172   Bill Moyers, 338.

173   Maya Angelou, On the Pulse of Morning, Inaguration of William Jefferson Clinton (Washington, D.C.: 20 Jan. 1993), Performance, 17 Oct. 2009, <http://www.hbci.com/~tgort/angelou.htm>.

174   Emma Lazarus, "The New Colossus," Liberty State Park, 28 Aug. 2009, <http://www.libertystatepark.com/emma.htm>.

175   Elizabeth Alexander, "Inaugural Poem: Praise Song for the Day," The New York Times, 20 Jan. 2009, 28 Aug. 2009, <http://www.nytimes.com/2009/01/20/us/politics/20text-poem.html?_r=1>.

176   Rita Dove, Qtd. in Moyers, Bill, The Language of Life (New York: Main Street Books, 1996), 112.

177   Langston Hughes, "Let America Be America Again," Poets.Org, 17 Oct. 2009, <http://www.poets.org/viewmedia.php/prmMID/15609>.

178   Ibid.

179   James Weldon Johnson, "Fifty Years, 1863-1913," Bartleby.Com: Great Books Online, 17 Oct. 2009, <http://www.bartleby.com/269/46.html>.

180   Sanchez, 148-149.

181   Pablo Neruda, "So Is My Life," Trans. Miguel Algarin, Medusa's Kitchen (17 Oct. 2009), <http://medusaskitchen.blogspot.com/2008/12/my-duty-my-song.html>.

182   Adrienne Rich, The Fact of a Doorframe: Poems Selected and New 1950-1984 (New York: W.W. Norton & Company, 1984), 264.

47781903R00094

Made in the USA
Lexington, KY
14 December 2015